£7-50

The Observer's Pocket Series

AIRCRAFT

The Observer Books

A POCKET REFERENCE SERIES
COVERING NATURAL HISTORY, TRANSPORT,
THE ARTS ETC

The Observer's Book of

AIRCRAFT

COMPILED BY

WILLIAM GREEN

WITH SILHOUETTES BY

DENNIS PUNNETT

DESCRIBING 185 AIRCRAFT
WITH 335 ILLUSTRATIONS

1971 Edition

FREDERICK WARNE & CO LTD
FREDERICK WARNE & CO INC
LONDON · NEW YORK

© FREDERICK WARNE & CO LTD
LONDON, ENGLAND
1971

Twentieth Edition 1971

Recommended by
THE AIR SCOUTS' DEPARTMENT
of
THE SCOUTS' ASSOCIATION

LIBRARY OF CONGRESS CATALOG CARD NO: 57–4425

ISBN 0 7232 1501 4

Printed in Great Britain

INTRODUCTION TO THE 1971 EDITION

In reviewing last year's edition of *The Observer's Book of Aircraft*, *BOAC News* remarked on the absence of the Boeing 707, commenting that its exclusion was a "rather curious omission". This comment prompts reiteration, in this 20th annual edition, of the intended purpose of *The Observer's Book*: the provision of a concise yearly reference source to the *latest* aircraft types to have flown or are expected to fly during the 12 months of the volume's currency, and to the most recent variants of established aeroplanes.

The criterion adopted in deciding the eligibility of aircraft to be included each year can be neither their production status nor their numerical importance. Such criteria would certainly dictate inclusion of the Boeing 707, as production is still running at one per month and more than 800 aircraft of the Boeing 707 family are serving with some 60 operators. However, the annual *Observer's Book* is not proffered as a reference to those aircraft most likely to be *seen* by the reader. If such was its intended task an *annual* edition would serve no purpose. The Boeing 707 first entered service in 1958 and, accordingly, made its début in the 1959 edition, reappearing each year in one form or another until, no new models having been evolved for several years, it was finally omitted from the 1969 edition. There can be no denying that this stalwart of the air lanes remains a highly important aircraft, but so do many other aeroplanes without the omission of which from the following pages no space would be available for later aeronautical débutantes.

It is precisely for this reason that two companion volumes—one devoted to military and the other to civil aircraft—were born some years ago. These, *The Observer's BASIC Books of Aircraft*, are revised and updated periodically, and are concerned not with the latest shapes in the world's skies but with those most likely to be seen, irrespective of production status or age. It is these companion volumes that should be consulted for such veterans as the Boeing 707 that have now passed from the pages of this annual.

In this 1971 edition the reader will find one important departure from previous practice, the use of metric in addition to Imperial measures.

The past year's aeronautical débutantes, such as the Grumman F-14 Tomcat shipboard fighter, the Corvette and Falcon 10 business executive aircraft, and the NAMC XC-1A and Fiat G 222 military transports, are joined in the following pages by the principal aircraft types scheduled to commence their test programmes during the course of 1971, including the C.212 Aviocar STOL utility transport, the Mitsubishi XT-2 advanced trainer, and the Dassault Mercure and VFW 614 short-haul airliners. All data have been updated, and all general-arrangement silhouettes thoroughly checked and, where necessary, revised.

AERFER-AERMACCHI AM.3C

Country of Origin: Italy.
Type: Battlefield surveillance and forward air control aircraft.
Power Plant: One 340 hp Piaggio-built Lycoming GSO-480-B1B6 six-cylinder horizontally-opposed engine.
Performance: (At normal loaded weight) Max. speed, 161 mph (260 km/h) at sea level, 173 mph (278 km/h) at 8,000 ft (2 440 m); max. cruise, 153 mph (246 km/h) at 8,000 ft (2 440 m); initial climb, 1,378 ft/min (7 m/sec); service ceiling, 27,560 ft (8 400 m); max. range with 30 min. reserves, 615 mls (990 km).
Weights: Empty equipped, 2,548 lb (1 156 kg); normal loaded, 3,307 lb (1 500 kg); max., 3,748 lb (1 700 kg).
Armament: Two underwing stores stations each stressed for loads up to 375 lb (170 kg), external armament including two pods each containing a pair of 7.62-mm guns with 1,000 rpg, or two Matra 125 packs each containing six 2.75-in rockets.
Status: First of two flying prototypes flown May 12, 1967, followed by second on August 22, 1968. Both initially fitted with Continental GTSIO-520-C engine (see 1968 edition) but re-engined with GSO-480-B1B6 as AM.3C in 1969. Production against initial export order for 20 aircraft to commence 1971.
Notes: AM.3C evaluated during 1970 by Italian Army and Air Force in competition with SIAI-Marchetti SM.1019 (see page 206).

AERFER-AERMACCHI AM.3C

Dimensions: Span, 38 ft 5$\frac{7}{8}$ in (11,73 m); length, 28 ft 7$\frac{3}{4}$ in (8,73 m); height, 8 ft 11 in (2,72 m); wing area, 204·944 sq ft (19,04 m²).

AERMACCHI M.B.326K

Country of Origin: Italy.

Type: Single-seat operational trainer and close-support aircraft.

Power Plant: One 4,000 lb (1 814 kg) Rolls-Royce Viper 632-43 turbojet.

Performance: (Estimated) Max. speed without external stores, 550 mph (885 km/h) at 19,685 ft (6 000 m); max. cruise, 497 mph (800 km/h); ferry range with two 90 Imp. gal. (409 l) underwing auxiliary tanks, 1,400 mls (2 250 km).

Weights: Empty equipped, 6,298 lb (2 857 kg); loaded (clean), 9,678 lb (4 390 kg); max., 12,000 lb (5 443 kg).

Armament: Two 30-mm DEFA or Aden cannon with 150 rpg. Six underwing stores stations of which four stressed for loads up to 1,000 lb (453,5 kg) and two for loads up to 750 lb (340 kg). Max. external ordnance load of 4,500 lb (2 040 kg).

Status: Prototype M.B.326K first flown August 22, 1970 with Viper 540 turbojet. Flight test programme with two prototypes scheduled for completion mid-1971 with production commencing before year's end.

Notes: M.B.326K is a single-seat dual-purpose derivative of the two-seat M.B.326G with the 3,410 lb (1 547 kg) Viper 540 turbojet (see 1970 edition). Apart from a more powerful turbojet, built-in cannon armament and a single-seat cockpit, the M.B.326K embodies some local strengthening of the forward fuselage structure, a high-flotation undercarriage, and provision for armour protection.

AERMACCHI M.B.326K

Dimensions: Span (over tip tanks), 35 ft $6\frac{3}{4}$ in (10,84 m); length, 34 ft $10\frac{7}{8}$ in (10,64 m); height, 12 ft $1\frac{3}{4}$ in (3,70 m); wing area, 207·958 sq ft (19,32 m^2).

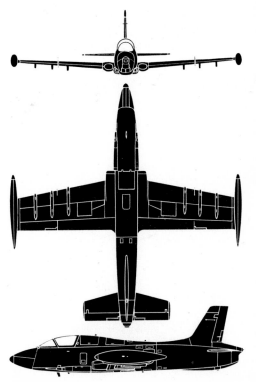

AERO L 39

Country of Origin: Czechoslovakia.

Type: Tandem two-seat basic and advanced trainer.

Power Plant: One 3,307 lb (1 500 kg) Walter Titan (Ivchenko AI-25V) turbofan.

Performance: Max. speed, 379 mph (610 km/h) at sea level, 454 mph (730 km/h) at 16,400 ft (5 000 m); range on internal fuel with 5% reserves, 680 mls (1 100 km), with tip-tanks and no reserves, 930 mls (1 500 km); initial climb, 3,740 ft/min (19 m/sec).

Weights: Empty, 6,283 lb (2 850 kg); normal loaded, 8,377 lb (3 800 kg); max. take-off, 9,480 lb (4 300 kg).

Status: First of five flying prototypes flown on November 4, 1968, and pre-production batch of 10 aircraft to be built during 1971 with full production commencing in 1972. Orders for 700 L 39s had been placed by beginning of 1971. Czechoslovak Air Force expected to receive up to 300 during 1972–75.

Notes: The L 39 is intended as a successor for the L 29 Delfin, and a 3,968-lb (1 800-kg) version of the Titan (AI-25VM) with a two-stage fan is under development for the production model. An afterburning Titan of some 4,410 lb (2 000 kg) is being developed for a light strike version of the L 39.

10

AERO L 39

Dimensions: Span, 29 ft 10¾ in (9,11 m); length, 39 ft 10⅔ in (12,12 m); height, 14 ft 4¼ in (4,38 m); wing area, 202·4 sq ft (18,8 m²).

AÉROSPATIALE SE 210 CARAVELLE 12

Country of Origin: France.
Type: Short- to medium-range commercial transport.
Power Plant: Two 14,500 lb (6 577 kg) Pratt & Whitney JT8D-9 turbofans.
Performance: Max. cruise at 25,000 ft (7 620 m), 504 mph (812 km/h) at 110,230 lb (50 000 kg); range with max. fuel at 32,000 ft (9 750 m), 2,423 mls (3 900 km) with 20,170 lb (9 150 kg) payload; range with max. payload (29,100 lb/13 200 kg), 1,693 mls (2 725 km).
Weights: Empty, 65,050 lb (29 500 kg); basic operational, 70,100 lb (31 800 kg); max., 123,460 lb (56 000 kg).
Accommodation: Normal flight crew of four and five-abreast seating for 118–128 tourist-class passengers, or mixed-class layout for 16 (four-abreast) first-class and 88 tourist-class passengers.
Status: Scheduled to be certificated early in 1971, the Caravelle 12 is the latest progressive development of the basic SE 210 airliner, and the first example of this lengthened model was flown for the first time on October 29, 1970. Seven Caravelle 12s are on order for the Danish independent operator Sterling Airways, a further four Caravelles of this type being on option.
Notes: Caravelle 12 is a long-body version of the Caravelle Super B (see 1966 edition) with an additional 6 ft 6$\frac{3}{4}$ in (2,00 m) fuselage section inserted ahead of the wing and a 3 ft 11$\frac{1}{2}$ in (1,21 m) section aft, plus local structural strengthening.

AÉROSPATIALE SE 210 CARAVELLE 12

Dimensions: Span, 112 ft 6½ in (34,30 m); length, 118 ft 10½ in (36,24 m); height, 29 ft 7 in (9,01 m); wing area, 1,579 sq ft (146,7 m²).

AÉROSPATIALE N 262C FRÉGATE

Country of Origin: France.

Type: Light short-range feederliner.

Power Plant: Two 1,360 shp Turboméca Bastan VIIA turboprops.

Performance: Max. speed, 260 mph (418 km/h); max. cruise, 254 mph (408 km/h) at 15,090 ft (4 600 m); normal cruise, 247 mph (397 km/h); range with max. fuel and no reserves, 1,490 mls (2 400 km), with max. payload and no reserves, 650 mls (1 050 km); initial climb, 1,496 ft/min (7,6 m/sec); service ceiling, 26,250 ft (8 000 m).

Weights: Empty equipped, 15,286 lb (6 934 kg); basic operational, 15,873 lb (7 200 kg); max. take-off, 23,370 lb (10 600 kg).

Accommodation: Basic flight crew of two and standard seating for 26 passengers in three-abreast rows (two to starboard and one to port of aisle). Alternative arrangement for 29 passengers.

Status: Development aircraft for C-series of the Frégate flown in July 1968 and series production of N 262C initiated 1970 alongside military counterpart, the N 262D for the *Armée de l'Air.*

Notes: The N 262C is similar to the initial production model of the Frégate, the N 262A, apart from its more powerful engines (the earlier model having Bastan VIs) and new wing-tips improving low-speed handling. The *Armée de l'Air* has accepted six A-series Frégates and, at the beginning of 1971, was in process of receiving 18 D-series aircraft.

AÉROSPATIALE N 262C FRÉGATE

Dimensions: Span, 71 ft 10¼ in (21,90 m); length, 63 ft 3 in (19,28 m); height, 20 ft 4 in (6,21 m); wing area, 592 sq ft (55,0 m²).

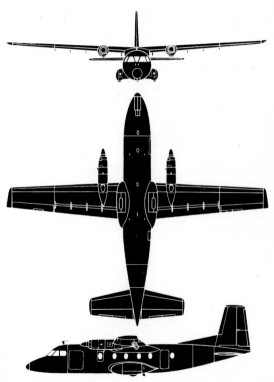

AÉROSPATIALE SN 600 CORVETTE

Country of Origin: France.

Type: Light business executive transport.

Power Plant: Two 2,205 lb (1 000 kg) Pratt & Whitney JT15D-1 turbofans.

Performance: (Estimated at max. take-off weight) Max. cruise, 466 mph (750 km/h) at 26,250 ft (8 000 m); econ. cruise, 391 mph (630 km/h) at 36,090 ft (11 000 m); range (with 13 passengers and 45 min reserves), 820 mls (1 320 km); initial climb, 3,346 ft/min (17 m/sec).

Weights: Empty equipped, 7,685 lb (3 486 kg); max. take-off, 12,500 lb (5 670 kg).

Accommodation: Normal flight crew of two and business executive arrangement for five–six passengers with alternative arrangements for 8–13 passengers.

Status: Prototype Corvette flown on July 16, 1970, and at the beginning of 1971 a decision concerning series production was awaiting completion of flight testing.

Notes: Two production versions of the Corvette are under consideration, one powered by JT15D-3 turbofans of 2,550 lb (1 156 kg) and the other by SNECMA-Turboméca Larzac turbofans of 2,304 lb (1 045 kg). In addition to business executive, air taxi, and third-level airline operations, the Corvette is also envisaged as a military liaison aircraft and is competing with the Dassault Falcon 10 (see page 66) for an order for the *Armée de l'Air*.

AÉROSPATIALE SN 600 CORVETTE

Dimensions: Span, 41 ft $11\frac{7}{8}$ in (12,80 m); length, 41 ft $11\frac{3}{4}$ in (12,79 m); height, 14 ft $3\frac{2}{3}$ in (4,36 m); wing area, 236·8 sq ft (22,0 m²).

AEROSTAR 601

Country of Origin: USA.

Type: Light business executive transport.

Power Plant: Two 290 hp Lycoming IO-540-G1B5 six-cylinder horizontally-opposed turbo-supercharged engines.

Performance: Max. cruise, 312 mph (502 km/h) at 25,000 ft (7 620 m), 300 mph (483 km/h) at 20,000 ft (6 095 m), 289 mph (465 km/h) at 15,000 ft (4 570 m); econ. cruise, 263 mph (423 km/h) at 20,000 ft (6 095 m), 251 mph (404 km/h) at 15,000 ft (4 570 m); range at 70% power with 30 min reserves at 50% power, 1,410 mls (2 265 km) at 20,000 ft (6 095 m); initial climb, 1,800 ft/min (9,1 m/sec); service ceiling, 30,000 ft (9 145 m).

Weights: Empty equipped, 3,725 lb (1 690 kg); max. take-off, 5,700 lb (2 585 kg).

Accommodation: Pilot and five passengers in individual seats. Full dual control.

Status: Production initiated as Ted Smith Aerostar in 1967, initial production Aerostar 600 and 601 flying on December 20, 1967 and July 9, 1968 respectively. Assets of Ted Smith Aircraft acquired by Butler Aviation International in February 1970, and aircraft-manufacturing subsidiary subsequently renamed Aerostar Aircraft Corporation. Production of Aerostar 601 and non-turbo-supercharged Aerostar 600 scheduled to attain 10 per month by mid-1971. Pressurised version under development as Aerostar 620.

AEROSTAR 601

Dimensions: Span, 34 ft 2½ in (10,43 m); length, 34 ft 9¾ in (10,61 m); height, 12 ft 1½ in (3,70 m); wing area, 170 sq ft (15,794 m²).

AESL AIRTOURER T6

Country of Origin: New Zealand.

Type: Light aerobatic trainer.

Power Plant: One 150 hp Lycoming O-320-E1A four-cylinder horizontally-opposed engine.

Performance: Max. speed, 164 mph (264 km/h) at sea level; max. cruise, 150 mph (241 km/h) at 4,000 ft (1 220 m); econ. cruise, 134 mph (216 km/h) at 5,000 ft (1 525 m); range, 670 mls (1 078 km); initial climb, 1,150 ft/min (5,84 m/sec); time to 10,000 ft (3 048 m), 11 min; service ceiling, 18,000 ft (5 486 m).

Weights: Empty equipped, 1,175 lb (532 kg); max. loaded, 1,850 lb (839 kg).

Accommodation: Two seats side-by-side with full dual controls.

Status: The Airtourer was initially built by Victa Limited in Australia, production being transferred in 1967 to Aero Engine Services Limited of New Zealand.

Notes: The Airtourer T6 is the military equivalent of the civil T5, four having been supplied to the RNZAF and two to the Singapore Armed Forces. Current Airtourers include the T1 with a 115 hp Lycoming O-235-C2A, the T2 and T4 with a 150 hp Lycoming O-320-E2A, and the T5 with an O-320-E1A and constant-speed airscrew.

AESL AIRTOURER T6

Dimensions: Span, 26 ft 0 in (7,92 m); length, 22 ft 0 in (6,71 m); height, 7 ft 0 in (2,13 m); wing area, 120 sq ft (11,148 m²).

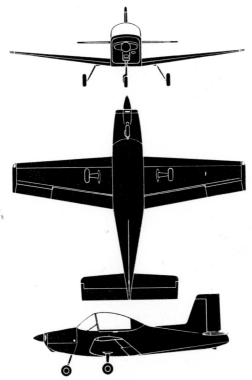

ANTONOV AN-22 ANTEI (COCK)

Country of Origin: USSR.

Type: Heavy military and commercial freighter.

Power Plant: Four 15,000 shp Kuznetsov NK-12MA turbo-props.

Performance: Max. speed, 460 mph (740 km/h); max. cruise, 422 mph (679 km/h); range with 99,208 lb (45 000 kg) payload, 6,835 mls (11 000 km) at 373 mph (600 km/h), with 176,370 lb (80 000 kg) payload, 3,107 mls (5 000 km) at 404 mph (650 km/h); cruise altitude, 26,250–32,800 ft (8 000–10 000 m).

Weights: Empty equipped, 251,327 lb (114 000 kg); max. take-off, 551,156 lb (250 000 kg).

Accommodation: Crew of five–six and cabin for 28–29 passengers between freight hold and flight deck. Freight hold can accommodate three tracked carriers for single Frog or twin Ganef surface-to-air missiles, self-propelled guns, etc.

Status: In production for both military and commercial use. First of five prototypes flown February 27, 1965, with first production deliveries following in the spring of 1967.

Notes: Capable of taking-off in fully loaded condition within 1,420 yards (1 300 m) and landing within 875 yards (800 m), the An-22 Antei (Antheus) is used extensively by the Soviet Air Forces and *Aeroflot*. The majority of An-22s now feature a reconfigured nose section (as illustrated on the opposite page) embodying two radars. During the course of 1970 the development of an airbus version for 300–350 passengers plus freight was reportedly continuing.

ANTONOV AN-22 ANTEI (COCK)

Dimensions: Span, 211 ft 3½ in (64,40 m); length, 189 ft 8 in (57,80 m); height, 41 ft 1 in (12,53 m); wing area, 3,713·55 sq ft (345 m²).

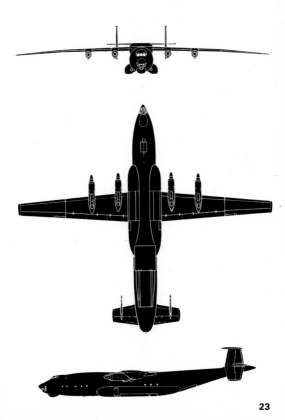

ANTONOV AN-26 (COKE)

Country of Origin: USSR.

Type: Short- to medium-range military and commercial freighter.

Power Plant: Two 2,820 eshp Ivchenko AI-24T turboprops and one (starboard nacelle) 1,984 lb (900 kg) Tumansky RU-19-300 auxiliary turbojet.

Performance: Max. speed, 335 mph (540 km/h) at 19,685 ft (6 000 m); normal cruise, 280 mph (450 km/h) at 19,685 ft (6 000 m); range cruise, 273 mph (440 km/h) at 22,965 ft (7 000 m): range with 3,307 lb (1 500 kg) payload and reserves, 1,553 mls (2 500 km), with 11,023 lb (5 000 kg) payload and reserves, 808 mls (1 300 km); service ceiling, 24,935 ft (7 600 m).

Weights: Empty equipped, 37,258 lb (16 914 kg); max. take-off, 52,911 lb (24 000 kg).

Accommodation: Normal crew of five with folding seats for up to 38 passengers/troops along main cabin walls. Direct rear loading for freight or vehicles and provision for air-dropping over rear ramp.

Status: Production deliveries for both military and commercial use reportedly commenced 1969.

Notes: Derivative of the commercial AN-24RT intended for both military and civil applications, the An-26 differs from An-24 variants in having a completely redesigned rear fuselage of "beavertail" type, and large paradrop observation blister to port below and aft of the flight deck.

ANTONOV AN-26 (COKE)

Dimensions: Span, 95 ft 10 in (29,20 m); length, 77 ft 2½ in (23,53 m); height, 27 ft 4 in (8,32 m); wing area, 779·95 sq ft (72,46 m²).

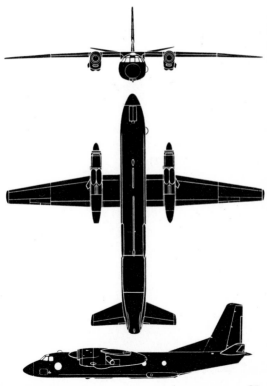

BAC 145 JET PROVOST T. MK. 5

Country of Origin: United Kingdom.
Type: Side-by-side two-seat primary and basic trainer.
Power Plant: One 2,500 lb (1 134 kg) Rolls-Royce Viper 202 turbojet.
Performance: Max. speed at 6,400 lb (2 903 kg), 409 mph (658 km/h) at sea level, 440 mph (708 km/h) at 25,000 ft (7 620 m); max. range with wingtip tanks, 900 mls (1 448 km) at 184 mph (296 km/h) at 35,000 ft (10 670 m); initial climb at 6,900 lb (3 130 kg), 4,000 ft/min (20,32 m/sec), at 7,600 lb (3 447 kg), 3,550 ft/min (18 m/sec); service ceiling, 36,750 ft (11 200 m) at 6,900 lb (3 130 kg).
Weights: Empty equipped, 5,490 lb (2 490 kg); normal take-off, 7,629 lb (3 460 kg), with full wingtip tanks, 8,524 lb (3 866 kg); max., 9,200 lb (4 173 kg).
Armament: Provision for two 7,62-mm FN machine guns with 550 rpg, and (T. Mk. 55) eight underwing stores stations of which two stressed for loads up to 500 lb (227 kg) and six for loads up to 200 lb (90,7 kg).
Status: First of two T. Mk. 5 prototypes flown on February 28, 1967, and deliveries to RAF against an order for 105 aircraft initiated September 1969. Five dual-role T. Mk. 55s delivered to Sudan.
Notes: A progressive development of the Hunting Jet Provost T. Mk. 4 which it is replacing in RAF service, the BAC 145 has redesigned wings for greater internal fuel capacity and longer fatigue life, and pressurised cabin. A more powerful derivative, the BAC 167, is illustrated and described on pages 32–33.

26

BAC 145 JET PROVOST T. MK. 5

Dimensions: Span, 35 ft 4 in (10,77 m); length, 34 ft 0 in (10,36 m); height, 10 ft 2 in (3,10 m); wing area, 213·7 sq ft (19,80 m²).

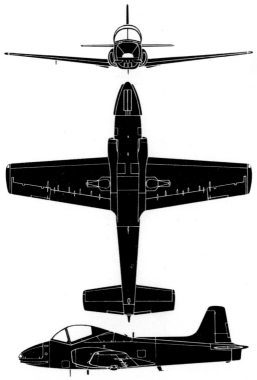

BAC LIGHTNING F. MK. 53

Country of Origin: United Kingdom.
Type: Single-seat interceptor, strike and reconnaissance fighter.
Power Plant: Two 11,100 lb (5 035 kg) dry and 16,300 lb (7 393 kg) reheat Rolls-Royce RB.146 Avon 302-C turbojets.
Performance: (Estimated in clean condition) Max. speed, 1,500 mph (2 415 km/h) or Mach 2·27 at 40,000 ft (12 190 m); long-range cruise, 595 mph (957 km/h) at 36,000–40,000 ft (10 970–12 190 m); initial climb, 50,000 ft/min (254 m/sec); time to 40,000 ft (12 190 m), 2·5 min; acceleration from Mach 1·0 to Mach 2·2, 3·5 min.
Weights: (Estimated) Max. loaded, 50,000 lb (22 680 kg).
Armament: Interchangeable packs containing equipment for two Red Top or Firestreak AAMs or 44 2-in (51-mm) rockets, plus two 30-mm Aden cannon with 120 rpg in ventral pack, plus two 1,000-lb (453,5-kg) bombs or two Matra 155 launchers for 18 68-mm SNEB rockets.
Status: First F. Mk. 53 flown November 1, 1966, and first delivery (to Saudi Arabia) December 4, 1967. Production of 34 for Saudi Arabia and 12 for Kuwait complete.
Notes: Multi-mission export version of RAF Lightning Mk. 6 interceptor, the definitive RAF single-seater. RAF received 44 Mk. 2, 58 Mk. 3 and 67 Mk. 6 single-seat Lightnings, 30 Mk. 2s having been modified as Mk. 2a version with Mk. 6 ventral pack.

BAC LIGHTNING F. MK. 53

Dimensions: Span, 34 ft 10 in (10,61 m); length (including probe), 55 ft 3 in (16,84 m); height, 19 ft 7 in (5,97 m); approx. wing area, 460 sq ft (42,73 m²).

BAC ONE-ELEVEN 475

Country of Origin: United Kingdom.
Type: Short- to medium-range commercial transport.
Power Plant: Two 12,550 lb (5 692 kg) Rolls-Royce Spey 512-14-DW turbofans.
Performance: Max. cruise, 548 mph (882 km/h) at 21,000 ft (6 400 m); econ. cruise, 507 mph (815 km/h) at 25,000 ft (7 620 m); range with reserves for 230 mls (370 km) diversion and 45 min, 2,095 mls (3 370 km), with capacity payload, 1,590 mls (2 560 km); initial climb rate at 345 mph (555 km/h), 2,350 ft/min (11,93 m/sec).
Weights: Basic operational, 51,814 lb (23 502 kg); max. take-off, 92,000 lb (41 730 kg).
Accommodation: Basic flight crew of two and up to 89 passengers. Typical mixed-class arrangement provides for 16 first-class (four-abreast) and 49 tourist-class (five-abreast) passengers.
Status: Aerodynamic prototype of One-Eleven 475 flown August 27, 1970, with certification and first production deliveries scheduled for June 1971.
Notes: The One-Eleven 475 combines the standard fuselage of the Series 400 with the redesigned wing and uprated engines of the Series 500 (see 1970 edition), coupling these with a low-pressure undercarriage to permit operation from gravel or low-strength sealed runways. The One-Eleven prototype flew on August 20, 1963, production models including the physically similar Series 200 and 300 with 10,330 lb (4 686 kg) Spey 506s and 11,400 lb (5 170 kg) Spey 511s, the Series 400 modified for US operation, and the Series 500 which is similar to the 475 apart from the fuselage.

BAC ONE-ELEVEN 475

Dimensions: Span, 93 ft 6 in (28,50 m); length, 93 ft 6 in (28,50 m); height, 24 ft 6 in (7,47 m); wing area, 1,031 sq ft (95,78 m²).

BAC 167 STRIKEMASTER

Country of Origin: United Kingdom.
Type: Side-by-side two-seat basic trainer and light attack and counter-insurgency aircraft.
Power Plant: One 3,410 lb (1 547 kg) Rolls-Royce Viper 535 turbojet.
Performance: Max. speed, 450 mph (724 km/h) at sea level, 472 mph (760 km/h) at 20,000 ft (6 096 m); range at 8,355 lb (3 789 kg), 725 mls (1 166 km), at 10,500 lb (4 762 kg), 1,238 mls (1 992 km), at 11,500 lb (5 216 kg), 1,382 mls (2 224 km); initial climb at 8,355 lb (3 789 kg), 5,250 ft/min (26,67 m/sec); time to 30,000 ft (9 150 m), 8 min 45 sec, to 40,000 ft (12 200 m), 15 min 30 sec.
Weights: Empty equipped, 5,850 lb (2 653 kg); normal take-off (pilot training), 8,355 lb (3 789 kg), (navigational training), 9,143 lb (4 147 kg); max., 11,500 lb (5 216 kg).
Armament: Provision for two 7,62-mm FN machine guns with 550 rpg and eight underwing stores stations for up to 3,000 lb (1 360 kg) of stores.
Status: Prototype Strikemaster flown October 26, 1967, with production deliveries following late 1968. Versions ordered and which differ only in equipment specified include Mk. 80 (Saudi Arabia), Mk. 81 (South Yemen), Mk. 82 (Muscat and Oman), Mk. 83 (Kuwait), Mk. 84 (Singapore), Mk. 85 (Kenya) and Mk. 86 (New Zealand). Total of 85 Strikemasters contracted for by beginning of 1971.
Notes: Derivative of BAC 145 (see pages 26–27).

BAC 167 STRIKEMASTER

Dimensions: Span, 35 ft 4 in (10,77 m); length, 34 ft 0 in (10,36 m); height, 10 ft 2 in (3,10 m); wing area, 213·7 sq ft (19,80 m²).

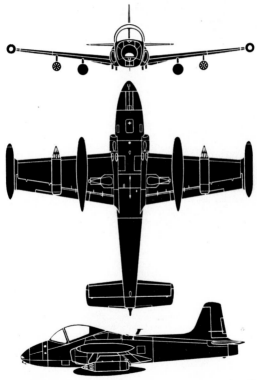

BAC-AÉROSPATIALE CONCORDE

Countries of Origin: United Kingdom and France.
Type: Long-range supersonic commercial transport.
Power Plant: Four 38,050 lb (17 259 kg) reheat Rolls-Royce/SNECMA Olympus 602 turbojets.
Performance: Max. cruise, 1,450 mph (2 330 km/h) or Mach 2·2 at 54,500 ft (16 000 m); max. range cruise, 1,350 mph (2 170 km/h) or Mach 2·05; max. fuel range with FAR reserves and 17,000-lb (7 710-kg) payload, 4,400 mls (7 080 km); max. payload range, 3,600 mls (5 790 km) at 616 mph (990 km/h) or Mach 0·93 at 30,000 ft (9 100 m), 4,020 mls (6 470 km) at 1,350 mph (2 170 km/h) or Mach 2·05 at 54,500 ft (16 000 m); initial climb, 5,000 ft/min (25,4 m/sec).
Weights: Operational empty, 169,000 lb (76 650 kg); max. take-off, 385,000 lb (90 720 kg).
Accommodation: Normal flight crew of three and economy-class seating for 128 passengers. Alternative high-density arrangement for 144 passengers.
Status: First and second prototypes flown March 2 and April 9, 1969 respectively. First of two pre-production aircraft scheduled to fly May 1971, the second following in October 1971, and first production aircraft in July 1972.
Notes: Both specification and general-arrangement silhouette apply to production Concorde, the prototypes featuring a shorter fuselage and differences in cockpit visor and wing profile. The Concorde reached Mach 2·0 on November 4, 1970, the prototypes having 34,700 lb (15 740 kg) Olympus 593-3Bs, and the definitive engine for the production model will be the Olympus 612 of 38,400 lb (17 418 kg).

BAC-AÉROSPATIALE CONCORDE

Dimensions: Span, 84 ft 0 in (25,60 m); length, 203 ft 8¾ in (62,10 m); height, 39 ft 10¼ in (12,15 m); wing area, 3,856 sq ft (358,25 m²).

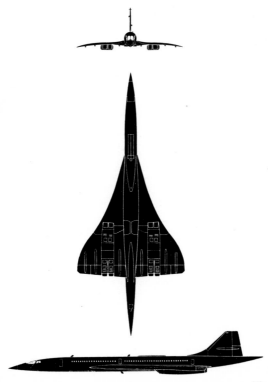

BEECHCRAFT 99A

Country of Origin: USA.

Type: Light commercial feederliner.

Power Plant: Two 680 shp Pratt & Whitney PT6A-27 turboprops.

Performance: Max. cruise, 284 mph (457 km/h) at 12,000 ft (3 650 m); econ. cruise, 279 mph (449 km/h) at 8,000 ft (2 440 m); range cruise, 216 mph (348 km/h) at 8,000 ft (2 440 m); max. fuel range, 887 mls (1 427 km) at 8,000 ft (2 440 m) with 45 min reserves at 279 mph (449 km/h), 1,048 mls (1 686 km) at 216 mph (348 km/h); initial climb, 1,700 ft/min (8,6 m/sec); service ceiling, 26,200 ft (7 985 m).

Weights: Empty equipped (standard 15-seater), 5,780 lb (2 621 kg); max. take-off, 10,400 lb (4 717 kg).

Accommodation: Normal flight crew of two and 15 passengers in individual seats on each side of central aisle. Optional 8-seat business executive transport arrangement. An 800-lb (363-kg) capacity ventral cargo pod (shown fitted above and on opposite page) may be carried.

Status: The prototype Model 99 was flown in July 1966 and the first production delivery followed on May 2, 1968, the 100th being delivered on April 28, 1969. The 36th production Model 99 served as a prototype for the Model 99A, deliveries of which began in 1969, and both versions remained in production at the beginning of 1971.

Notes: Standard Model 99 has 550 shp PT6A-20 turboprops.

BEECHCRAFT 99A

Dimensions: Span, 45 ft $10\frac{1}{2}$ in (14,00 m); length, 44 ft $6\frac{3}{4}$ in (13,58 m); height, 14 ft $4\frac{1}{3}$ in (4,40 m); wing area, 279·7 sq ft (25,985 m²).

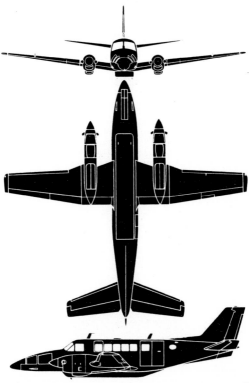

BEECHCRAFT MUSKETEER SUPER R

Country of Origin: USA.

Type: Light cabin monoplane.

Power Plant: One 200 hp Lycoming IO-360-A2B four-cylinder horizontally-opposed engine.

Performance: Max. speed, 170 mph (274 km/h) at sea level; cruise at 75% power, 162 mph (261 km/h) at 7,000 ft (2 135 m), at 65% power, 154 mph (248 km/h) at 10,000 ft (3 050 m), at 55% power, 140 mph (225 km/h) at 10,000 ft (3 050 m); range with 45 min reserves, 657 mls (1 057 km) at 75% power, 824 mls (1 326 km) at 65% power, 880 mls (1 416 km) at 55% power; initial climb, 910 ft/min (4,6 m/sec); service ceiling, 15,000 ft (4 570 m).

Weights: Empty equipped, 1,625 lb (737 kg); max. take-off, 2,750 lb (1 247 kg).

Accommodation: Pilot and three to five passengers in pairs.

Status: The Model 23 Musketeer was first flown on October 23, 1961, initial production deliveries following in the autumn of 1962. Design reappraisal resulted in a new range of Musketeers in 1965, and the Musketeer Super R, introduced into the 1970 range, differs from earlier models primarily in having a retractable undercarriage.

Notes: The Super R is essentially similar to the Super apart from its undercarriage, other current models being the Custom four-seater with a 180 hp Lycoming O-360-A2G and the two-seat Sport with a 150 hp Lycoming O-320-E2C.

BEECHCRAFT MUSKETEER SUPER R

Dimensions: Span, 32 ft 9 in (9,98 m); length, 25 ft 1 in (7,65 m); height, 8 ft 3 in (2,51 m); wing area, 146 sq ft (13,57 m²).

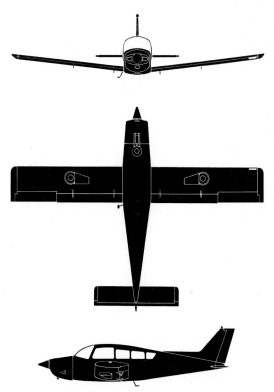

BERIEV BE-12 TCHAIKA (MAIL)

Country of Origin: USSR.

Type: Maritime patrol and reconnaissance amphibian.

Power Plant: Two 4,190 eshp Ivchenko AI-20D turbo-props.

Performance: (Estimated) Max. speed, 380 mph (610 km/h) at 10,000 ft (3 050 m); max. cruise, 340 mph (547 km/h) at 15,000 ft (4 570 m); normal patrol speed, 200–250 mph (320–400 km/h) at 5,000 ft (1 525 m); initial climb at normal loaded weight, 3,000 ft/min (15,2 m/sec); service ceiling, 37,000 ft (11 280 m); max. range, 2,500 mls (4 025 km).

Weights: (Estimated) Max. take-off, 60,000–65,000 lb (27 220–29 485 kg).

Armament: Underwing stores stations for homing torpedoes, depth bombs, mines or rockets. Internal stowage for sono-buoys.

Status: Reportedly flown in prototype form in 1960, the Be-12 is believed to have entered service with the Soviet Navy during 1965–66.

Notes: The largest amphibian flying boat currently in service, the Be-12 Tchaika (Gull) is standard equipment with the Soviet Navy maritime patrol units and established a number of FAI-recognised records for aircraft in its class during 1964–70.

BERIEV BE-12 TCHAIKA (MAIL)

Dimensions: (Estimated) Span, 108 ft 0 in (32,9 m); length, 96 ft 0 in (29,26 m); height, 23 ft 0 in (7,01 m); wing area, 1,030 sq ft (95,69 m²).

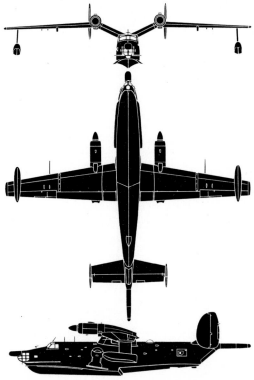

BERIEV BE-30 (CUFF)

Country of Origin: USSR.

Type: Light short-range commercial feederliner.

Power Plant: Two 970 eshp Glushenkov TVD-10 turbo-props.

Performance: Max. speed, 304 mph (490 km/h); max. cruise, 286 mph (460 km/h) at 6,500 ft (1 980 m); range with 1,984-lb (900-kg) payload and 30 min reserves, 620 mls (1 000 km) at 236 mph (380 km/h), with 2,755-lb (1 250-kg) payload, 373 mls (600 km).

Weights: Empty equipped, 7,937 lb (3 600 kg); max. take-off, 12,919 lb (5 860 kg).

Accommodation: Normal flight crew of two and standard arrangement for 14 passengers in pairs in individual seats on each side of central aisle. Proposed high-density arrangements for 21–23 passengers.

Status: First prototype Be-30 flown (with ASh-21 piston engines) on March 3, 1967, followed by definitive series prototype on July 18, 1968. The Be-30 was scheduled to enter service with *Aeroflot* during the course of 1970.

Notes: Designed specifically for use by *Aeroflot* over local service routes not justifying use of the larger An-24, and capable of operating from short grass strips or gravel runways, the Be-30 is also being developed for geological survey and other tasks. It is also convertible for use as a freighter or air ambulance, accommodating nine stretcher cases and six seated casualties in the latter role.

BERIEV BE-30 (CUFF)

Dimensions: Span, 55 ft 9¼ in (17,00 m); length, 51 ft 6 in (15,70 m); height, 17 ft 0¾ in (5,20 m); wing area, 344·445 sq ft (32,0 m²).

BOEING MODEL 727-100C

Country of Origin: USA.

Type: Medium-range commercial convertible cargo-passenger transport.

Power Plant: Three 14,000 lb (6 350 kg) Pratt & Whitney JT8D-7 turbofans.

Performance: Max. speed, 630 mph (1 014 km/h) at 21,600 ft (6 585 m); max. cruise, 605 mph (974 km/h) at 19,000 ft (5 800 m); econ. cruise, 570 mph (917 km/h) at 30,000 ft (9 150 m); range with max. fuel, 2,650 mls (4 265 km), with max. payload, 1,900 mls (3 058 km); initial climb, 3,150 ft/min (16 m/sec); service ceiling, 37,400 ft (11 400 m).

Weights: Operational empty, 89,537 lb (40 613 kg); standard max. take-off, 160,000 lb (72 570 kg); optional max. take-off, 169,000 lb (76 655 kg).

Accommodation: Normal flight crew of three. Typical payloads comprise 94 mixed-class passengers, 52 passengers plus 22,700 lb (10 295 kg) of cargo, or 38,000 lb (17 236 kg) of cargo. Conversion from mixed passenger/cargo to all-cargo configuration is possible in less than two hours.

Status: First Model 727-100 flown February 9, 1963, first delivery (to United) following on October 29, 1963. Model 727-200 (see 1970 edition) flown July 27, 1967, with first delivery following (to Northeast) on December 11, 1967. Approximately 825 of all versions delivered by beginning of 1971.

Notes: Model 727-100C is identical to -100 apart from strengthened freight floor and cargo door. The -100QC uses palletised passenger seats and galleys.

BOEING MODEL 727-100C

Dimensions: Span, 108 ft 0 in (32,92 m); length, 133 ft 2 in (40,59 m); height, 34 ft 0 in (10,36 m); wing area, 1,700 sq ft (157,9 m²).

BOEING MODEL 737-200C

Country of Origin: USA.

Type: Short-range commercial convertible cargo—passenger transport.

Power Plant: Two 14,500 lb (6 575 kg) Pratt & Whitney JT8D-9 turbofans.

Performance: Max. speed, 586 mph (943 km/h) at 23,500 ft (7 165 m); max. cruise, 568 mph (915 km/h) at 21,900 ft (6 675 m); econ. cruise, 525 mph (845 km/h) at 30,000 ft (9 145 m); range with max. fuel and reserves for 200-mile diversion and 45 min, 2,210 mls (3 555 km), max. payload and similar reserves, 2,135 mls (3 435 km).

Weights: Operational empty (all cargo), 59,109 lb (26 805 kg), (all passenger), 62,436 lb (28 315 kg); max. take-off, 114,500 lb (51 925 kg).

Accommodation: Normal flight crew of two and up to 119 passengers in six-abreast seating in all-passenger configuration, or up to 34,270 lb (15 544 kg) cargo in all-cargo configuration, or various combinations of passengers and cargo.

Status: First Model 737-100 flown on April 9, 1967 (see 1967 edition), followed by first -200 on August 8, 1967. Approximately 260 Model 737s of all versions delivered by beginning of 1971.

Notes: All aircraft delivered after May 1971 will be completed to the so-called "Advanced 737-200/C/QC" standard (to which specification refers), embodying improvements in range and short-field performance.

46

BOEING MODEL 737-200C

Dimensions: Span, 93 ft 0 in (28,35 m); length, 100 ft 0 in (30,48 m); height, 37 ft 0 in (11,28 m); wing area, 980 sq ft (91,05 m²).

BOEING MODEL 747-100

Country of Origin: USA.
Type: Long-range large-capacity commercial transport.
Power Plant: Four 43,500 lb (19 730 kg) Pratt & Whitney JT9D-3 turbofans.
Performance: Max. speed at 600,000 lb (272 155 kg), 595 mph (958 km/h) at 30,000 ft (9 150 m); long-range cruise, 589 mph (948 km/h) at 35,000 ft (10 670 m); range with max. fuel and FAR reserves, 7,080 mls (11 395 km), with 374 passengers, 5,790 mls (9 138 km); cruise ceiling, 45,000 ft (13 715 m).
Weights: Operational empty, 348.816 lb (158 220 kg); max. take-off, 710,000 lb (322 050 kg).
Accommodation: Normal flight crew of three and basic accommodation for 66 first-class and 308 economy-class passengers. Alternative layouts for 447 or 490 economy-class passengers in nine-abreast and 10-abreast seating respectively.
Status: First Model 747-100 flown on February 9, 1969, and first commercial services (by Pan American) inaugurated January 22, 1970. The first Model 747-200 (747B), the 88th aircraft off the assembly line, flown October 11, 1970.
Notes: Principal production versions of the Model 747 are currently the -100 and -200 series, the latter having greater fuel capacity and maximum take-off weight increased to 775,000 lb (351 540 kg), convertible passenger/cargo and all-cargo versions of the -200 series (alias Model 747B) being designated 747C and 747F respectively.

48

BOEING MODEL 747-100

Dimensions: Span, 195 ft 8 in (59,64 m); length, 231 ft 4 in (70,51 m); height, 63 ft 5 in (19,33 m); wing area, 5,685 sq ft (528,15 m²).

BREGUET 1150 ATLANTIC

Country of Origin: France.

Type: Long-range maritime patrol aircraft.

Power Plant: Two 6,105 ehp Hispano-built Rolls-Royce Tyne R.Ty.20 Mk. 21 turboprops.

Performance: Max. speed, 409 mph (658 km/h); max. cruise, 363 mph (584 km/h) at 19,685 ft (6 000 m), 342 mph (550 km/h) at 26,250 ft (8 000 m); range cruise, 311 mph (500 km/h) at 26,250 ft (8 000 m); max. endurance cruise, 195 mph (320 km/h); loiter endurance at range of 620 mls (1 000 km), 12 hrs; max. endurance, 18 hrs; range with 10% reserves, 4,950 mls (7 970 km); max. range, 5,590 mls (9 000 km); initial climb, 2,450 ft/min (12,44 m/sec); service ceiling, 32,800 ft (10 000 m).

Weights: Empty, 52,900 lb (24 000 kg); max. take-off, 95,900 lb (43 500 kg).

Armament: Nine 400-lb (181,4-kg) Mk. 44 acoustic torpedoes or four 1,124-lb (510-kg) L4 torpedoes plus single nuclear depth charge internally, and four AS.12 missiles beneath wings.

Accommodation: Crew of 12 of which seven accommodated in central operations compartment.

Status: First of three prototypes flown October 21, 1961, and production against total orders for 87 (40 for France, 20 for Germany, 18 for Italy and nine for the Netherlands) scheduled to continue until early 1973.

Notes: Built by French-German-Belgian-Dutch consortium.

BREGUET 1150 ATLANTIC

Dimensions: Span, 119 ft $1\frac{1}{4}$ in (36,30 m); length, 104 ft $1\frac{1}{2}$ in (31,75 m); height, 37 ft $1\frac{3}{4}$ in (11,33 m); wing area, 1,295·33 sq ft (120,34 m²).

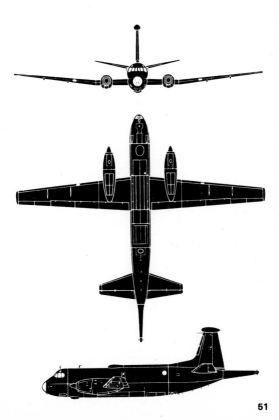

BRITTEN-NORMAN ISLANDER SRS.2

Country of Origin: United Kingdom.
Type: Light utility transport.
Power Plant: Two 260 hp Lycoming O-540-E4C5 six-cylinder horizontally-opposed engines.
Performance: (At 6,000 lb/2 722 kg) Max. speed, 171 mph (275 km/h) at sea level; cruise at 75% power, 161 mph (258 km/h) at 7,000 ft (2 140 m), at 67% power, 159 mph (255 km/h) at 9,000 ft (2 750 m), at 59% power, 154 mph (247 km/h) at 13,000 ft (3 960 m); range with max. fuel and 30 min reserves, 810 mls (1 300 km), with max. payload and same reserves, 425 mls (670 km); initial climb, 1,150 ft/min (5,85 m/sec); service ceiling, 16,500 ft (5 040 m).
Weights: Empty equipped, 3,588 lb (1 627 kg); max. take-off, 6,300 lb (2 857 kg).
Accommodation: Flight crew of one or two and 8–9 passengers on bench-type seats, or two casualty stretchers and two attendants for ambulance role.
Status: Prototype flown June 12, 1965, followed by first production aircraft on August 20, 1966. Assembly undertaken by IRMA in Rumania, the first Rumanian-assembled Islander having flown on August 11, 1969. Approximately 250 Islanders delivered by beginning of 1971.
Notes: Series 2 embodying detail improvements replaced Series 1 from June 1969. Optional 21 Imp gal (100 l) auxiliary tanks in extended wingtips (illustrated opposite) increases span to 53 ft 0 in (16,15 m).

BRITTEN-NORMAN ISLANDER SRS.2

Dimensions: Span, 49 ft 0 in (14,94 m); length, 35 ft 8 in (10,87 m); height, 13 ft 8 in (4,16 m); wing area, 325 sq ft (30,2 m²).

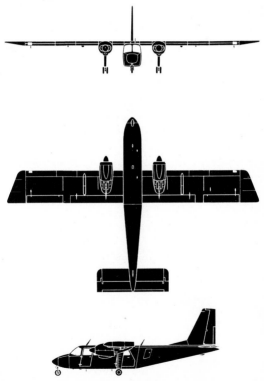

BRITTEN-NORMAN ISLANDER SRS.3

Country of Origin: United Kingdom.

Type: Light utility transport and feederliner.

Power Plant: Three 260 hp Lycoming O-540-E4C5 six-cylinder horizontally-opposed engines.

Performance: Max. speed, 192 mph (309 km/h) at sea level; cruise at 75% power, 185 mph (298 km/h) at 6,500 ft (1 980 m), at 59% power, 175 mph (281 km/h) at 13,000 ft (3 962 m); range at 67% power with 10% reserves plus 45 min hold (16 passengers), 200 mls (322 km).

Weights: Empty equipped, 5,020 lb (2 277 kg); max. take-off, 9,000 lb (4 082 kg).

Accommodation: Flight crew of one or two and 16–17 passengers on bench-type seats.

Status: Prototype Islander Srs. 3 (modification of second Srs.1 prototype) flown September 11, 1970. Production deliveries expected to commence during second half of 1971.

Notes: The Islander Srs. 3 possesses 75% commonality with the current production Srs.2 (see pages 52–53) from which it differs primarily in having a 90-in (2,286-m) addition of standard parallel fuselage section forward of the wing, redesigned tail surfaces carrying a third engine and embodying an electrically-actuated variable-incidence tailplane, a new undercarriage and some strengthening of the wing centre section. The wingtip auxiliary fuel tanks optional on the Srs.2 are standardised for the Srs.3. The Srs.3 is intended primarily as a commuter transport for third-level airlines.

BRITTEN-NORMAN ISLANDER SRS.3

Dimensions: Span, 53 ft 0 in (16,15 m); length, 43 ft 9 in (13,33 m); height, 13 ft 4 in (4,06 m); wing area, 337 sq ft (31,25 m²).

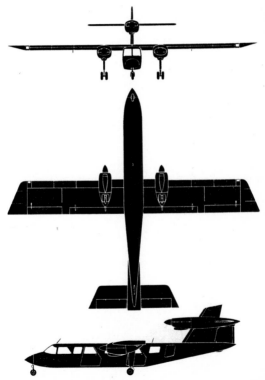

BRITTEN-NORMAN NYMPH 160

Country of Origin: United Kingdom.
Type: Light cabin monoplane.
Power Plant: One 160 hp Lycoming O-320 four-cylinder horizontally-opposed engine.
Performance: Max. speed, 135 mph (217 km/h) at sea level; max. cruise, 130 mph (209 km/h) at 7,500 ft (2 285 m); max. range, 520 mls (835 km); initial climb, 700 ft/min (3,5 m/sec); service ceiling, 12,000 ft (3 660 m).
Weights: Empty, 1,250 lb (566 kg); max. take-off, 2,350 lb (1 065 kg).
Accommodation: Side-by-side individual seats in pairs for pilot and three passengers.
Status: Prototype flown on May 17, 1969, with 115 hp Lycoming O-235-C1B as Nymph 115 and re-engined during summer 1970 as Nymph 160. Production plans delayed but development continuing on low-priority basis at beginning of 1971.
Notes: The Nymph has been designed for supply in kit form and subsequent assembly by authorised maintenance and repair organisations and other approved agencies. The kits will be supplied with all metal shaped and cut to size, and no special jigs or tools will be required for assembly. Versions with 115, 130 and 160 hp engines are envisaged.

BRITTEN-NORMAN NYMPH 160

Dimensions: Span, 39 ft 3$\frac{7}{8}$ in (11,98 m); length, 23 ft 7$\frac{3}{4}$ in (7,20 m); height, 9 ft 6 in (2,90 m); wing area, 169 sq ft (15,7 m²).

CANADAIR CL-215-102

Country of Origin: Canada.
Type: Multi-purpose utility amphibian.
Power Plant: Two 2,100 hp Pratt & Whitney R-2800-83AM2AH 18-cylinder radial engines.
Performance: Max. cruise at 41,000 lb (18 597 kg), 173 mph (278 km/h) at 8,000 ft (2 438 m); range with 3,500-lb (1 587-kg) payload, 1,000 mls (1 610 km); initial climb at 36,000 lb (16 329 kg), 943 ft/min (4,79 m/sec).
Weights: Empty, 25,900 lb (11 748 kg); typical operational empty, 27,000 lb (12 247 kg); max. take-off (utility), 36,000 lb (16 329 kg), (water bomber), 43,500 lb (19 731 kg).
Accommodation: Normal flight crew of two, and (utility version) standard accommodation for 19 passengers in main cabin.
Status: First of two prototypes flown October 23, 1967. Delivery of 10 to the French *Service de la Protection Civile* completed 1970, and deliveries of 15 to the Quebec Government in process at beginning of 1971.
Notes: Development of the CL-215 was initiated and partly funded by the Government of Quebec for the water-bombing of forest fires, and the amphibian performs the same task with France's *Protection Civile*, the basic version, described above and illustrated, being designated CL-215-102. A proposed growth version has R-2800-CB-17 engines.

CANADAIR CL-215-102

Dimensions: Span, 93 ft 10 in (28,60 m); length, 65 ft $0\frac{1}{4}$ in (19,82 m); height, 29 ft $5\frac{1}{2}$ in (8,98 m); wing area, 1,080 sq ft (100,33 m²).

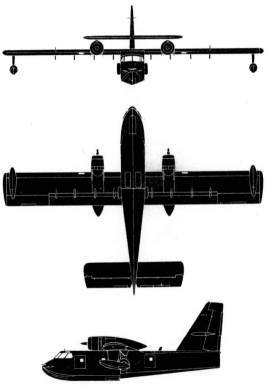

CASA C.212 AVIOCAR

Country of Origin: Spain.
Type: STOL utility transport.
Power Plant: Two 755 eshp Garrett-AiResearch TPE 331-201 turboprops.
Performance: (Estimated) Max. cruise (80% power), 202 mph (325 km/h) at 10,000 ft (3 050 m); range cruise, 186 mph (300 km/h); max. range with reserves of 5% plus 20 min hold, 1,193 mls (1 920 km), with 4,410 lb (2 000 kg) cargo and same reserves, 447 mls (720 km); initial climb, 1,655 ft/min (8,4 m/sec).
Weights: Empty equipped, 7,160 lb (3 250 kg); max. take-off, 13,230 lb (6 000 kg).
Accommodation: Flight crew of two and (commercial version) 18 passengers with alternative high-density arrangement for 21 passengers. Ten casualty stretchers, three sitting casualties plus medical attendants may be accommodated for the ambulance role, and the military version will carry 15 paratroops and a jumpmaster.
Status: First of two prototypes scheduled to fly early 1971. Pre-series of 12 aircraft planned with production deliveries commencing 1973.
Notes: The Aviocar has been designed primarily for operation by the Spanish Air Force, this service having a requirement for some 60 aircraft to replace the Junkers Ju 52/3m and Douglas C-47. The Aviocar features a rear loading ramp which may be opened in flight to facilitate paradrops.

CASA C.212 AVIOCAR

Dimensions: Span, 62 ft 4 in (19,00 m); length, 49 ft 8½ in (15,15 m); height, 20 ft 8¾ in (6,32 m); wing area, 430·556 sq ft (40 m²).

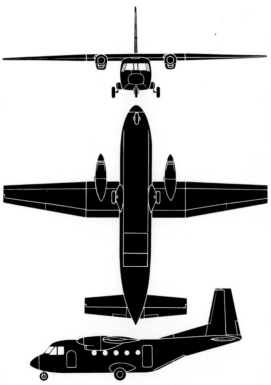

CESSNA 421B GOLDEN EAGLE

Country of Origin: USA.

Type: Light commercial and business executive transport.

Power Plant: Two 375 hp Continental GTSIO-520-D six-cylinder horizontally-opposed engines.

Performance: Max. speed, 238 mph (383 km/h) at sea level, 283 mph (455 km/h) at 18,000 ft (5 485 m); max. cruise at 75% power, 234 mph (376 km/h) at 10,000 ft (3 050 m), 270 mph (434 km/h) at 25,000 ft (7 620 m); max. range without reserves, 1,628 mls (2 620 km) at 192 mph (309 km/h) at 10,000 ft (3 050 m), 1,742 mls (2 803 km) at 235 mph (378 km/h) at 25,000 ft (7 620 m); initial climb, 1,950 ft/min (9,9 m/sec); service ceiling, 31,800 ft (9 693 m).

Weights: Empty, 4,359 lb (1 977 kg); max. take-off, 7,250 lb (3 280 kg).

Accommodation: Normal flight crew of two and six passengers in separate main cabin.

Status: Prototype Model 421 flown October 14, 1965, initial deliveries following May 1967 (see 1968 edition). Deliveries of improved Model 421B Golden Eagle commenced mid-1970, and 1,415 Cessna 400 series (including 391 Model 421s) produced by 1971.

Notes: Model 421 is one of two pressurised aircraft in the Cessna 400 family, the other being the Model 414 with similar wings to those of the unpressurised Model 402A (see 1970 edition) and 310 hp TSIO-520-J engines. Model 421B introduces new extended nose.

62

CESSNA 421B GOLDEN EAGLE

Dimensions: Span, 41 ft 10¼ in (12,76 m); length, 36 ft 1 in (11,00 m); height, 11 ft 7 in (3,53 m); wing area, 211·65 sq ft (19,66 m²).

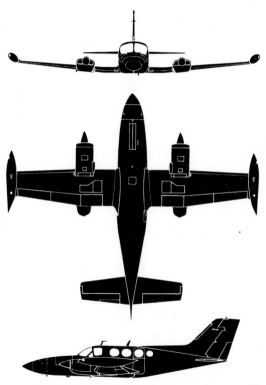

CESSNA MODEL 500 CITATION

Country of Origin: USA.

Type: Light business executive transport.

Power Plant: Two 2,200 lb (1 000 kg) Pratt & Whitney JT15D-1 turbofans.

Performance: Max. speed, 402 mph (647 km/h) at 26,400 ft (8 046 m); max. cruise, 400 mph (644 km/h) at 25,400 ft (7 740 m); range with eight persons and 45 min reserves at 90% cruise thrust, 1,397 mls (2 248 km), with two persons and same reserves at 90% cruise thrust, 1,502 mls (2 417 km); initial climb, 3,350 ft/min (17 m/sec); service ceiling, 38,400 ft (11 704 m).

Weights: Empty (excluding avionics), 5,408 lb (2 453 kg); max. take-off, 10,350 lb (4 695 kg).

Accommodation: Crew of two on separate flight deck and alternative arrangements for five or six passengers in main cabin.

Status: First prototype flown on September 15, 1969, and first production Citation scheduled for completion in April 1971. Customer deliveries to commence late 1971 with 60–80 to be completed during first year of production.

Notes: The Citation places emphasis on short-field performance, balanced field length being 2,950 ft (899 m) and take-off distance to clear a 35-ft (10,7-m) obstacle being 2,300 ft (701 m), enabling the aircraft to use some 2,300 US airfields. The Citation is being offered in basic standard configuration or as a complete business aircraft package with factory-installed interior and avionics, ground and flight training and one year of maintenance service.

CESSNA MODEL 500 CITATION

Dimensions: Span, 43 ft 8½ in (13,32 m); length, 43 ft 6 in (13,26 m); height, 14 ft 3¾ in (4,36 m); wing area, 260 sq ft (24,15 m²).

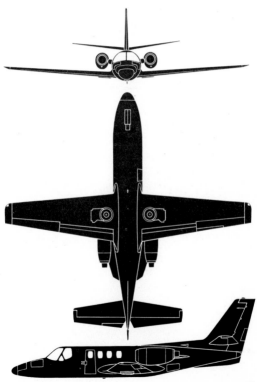

DASSAULT FALCON 10

Country of Origin: France.

Type: Light business executive transport.

Power Plant: Two 3,230 lb (1 465 kg) Garrett-AiResearch TFE 731-2 turbofans.

Performance: (Estimated) Max. cruise, 559 mph (900 km/h) at 25,000 ft (7 620 m); range with four passengers and 45 min reserves, 2,225 mls (3 580 km), with seven passengers and same reserves, 2,130 mls (3 430 km); absolute ceiling, 45,200 ft (13 780 m).

Weights: Empty equipped, 9,710 lb (4 404 kg); max. take-off, 18,298 lb (8 300 kg).

Accommodation: Flight crew of two and normal seating for four or seven passengers.

Status: First prototype flown December 1, 1970, and first production deliveries scheduled for late 1972. More than 50 Falcon 10s ordered by beginning of 1971.

Notes: The Falcon 10 is basically a scaled-down version of the Falcon 20 (see pages 68–69), and is to be offered with either the TFE 731-2 or the SNECMA-Turboméca Larzac turbofan, the latter being rated at 2,315 lb (1 050 kg). The first prototype Falcon 10 is flying with 2,950-lb (1 340-kg) General Electric CJ610-6 turbojets and the second prototype is to commence flight testing with Larzac turbofans. A military crew training and liaison version of the Falcon 10 is competing with the Aérospatiale SN 600 Corvette (see pages 16–17) to fulfil an *Armée de l'Air* requirement, an order for some 45 examples of the selected aircraft being anticipated.

DASSAULT FALCON 10

Dimensions: Span, 43 ft 0 in (13,10 m); length, 44 ft 11 in (13,69 m); height, 14 ft 3 in (4,37 m); wing area, 242·19 sq ft (22,5 m²).

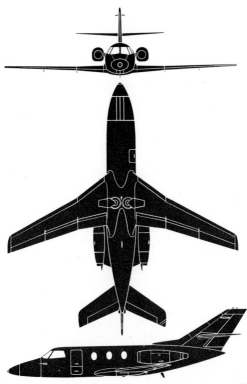

DASSAULT FALCON 20 SERIES F

Country of Origin: France.

Type: Light business executive transport.

Power Plant: Two 4,315 lb (1 983 kg) General Electric CF700-2D-2 turbofans.

Performance: Max. speed, 404 mph (650 km/h) at sea level, 449 mph (722 km/h) at 22,965 ft (7 000 m); max. cruise, 535 mph (860 km/h); range with eight passengers and 45 min reserves, 2,300 mls (3 580 km) at 39,370 ft (12 000 m); max. operating altitude, 42,650 ft (13 000 m).

Weights: Empty, 15,972 lb (7 245 kg); max. take-off, 28,660 lb (13 000 kg).

Accommodation: Normal flight crew of two and standard arrangement for eight passengers in individual seats. Alternative arrangements available for 10—14 passengers.

Status: First Falcon 20 (alias Mystère 20) flown May 4, 1963, followed by first production aircraft on January 1, 1965. The prototype Series F (172nd airframe) flown May 1969 and first production example of this series delivered June 1970. More than 200 Falcon 20s delivered by beginning of 1971 against 270 firm orders.

Notes: Current production version of the Falcon 20, the Series F, differs from the Series E that it supplants in having wing high-lift devices to reduce field length and increased fuel tankage. The Series 30 for 1972 delivery will have Garrett-AiResearch ATF 3A turbofans, a lengthened fuselage, enlarged fin and new electrics.

DASSAULT FALCON 20 SERIES F

Dimensions: Span, 53 ft 6 in (16,30 m); length, 56 ft 3 in (17,15 m); height, 17 ft 5 in (5,32 m); wing area, 440 sq ft (41 m²).

DASSAULT MERCURE

Country of Origin: France.

Type: Short-range commercial transport.

Power Plant: Two 15,500 lb (7 030 kg) Pratt & Whitney JT8D-15 turbofans.

Performance: (Estimated) Max. cruise, 576 mph (927 km/h) at 22,000 ft (6 705 m); econ. cruise, 572 mph (920 km/h) at 24,935 ft (7 600 m); long-range cruise, 512 mph (825 km/h) at 35,100 ft (10 700 m); range with max. fuel, ATA reserves and 25,397-lb (11 520-kg) payload, 1,035 mls (1 670 km), with max. payload of 36,508 lb (16 560 kg) and same reserves, 446 mls (720 km).

Weights: Empty, 56,527 lb (25 640 kg); empty equipped, 60,854 lb (27 603 kg); max. take-off, 114,640 lb (52 000 kg).

Accommodation: Normal flight crew of two and basic accommodation for 134 tourist-class passengers in six-abreast seating. Typical mixed-class arrangement for 16 first-class (four-abreast) and 100 tourist-class (six-abreast) passengers. High-density arrangements for up to 155 passengers.

Status: First prototype scheduled to fly May 1971, followed by second prototype in January 1972 with certification January 1973. First delivery (to Air Inter) scheduled for April 1973.

Notes: Mercure is being built by international consortium under Dassault leadership, including Italian, Belgian, Spanish and Swiss companies. First prototype to be powered by 15,000 lb (6 805 kg) JT8D-11s.

DASSAULT MERCURE

Dimensions: Span, 100 ft 3 in (30,55 m); length, 111 ft 6 in (34,00 m); height, 37 ft 3¼ in (11,36 m); wing area, 1,250 sq ft (116 m²).

DASSAULT MILAN S

Country of Origin: France.

Type: Single-seat multi-purpose fighter.

Power Plant: One 11,023 lb (5 000 kg) dry and 15,873 lb (7 200 kg) reheat SNECMA Atar 9K-50 turbojet.

Performance: Max. speed (clean), 865 mph (1 390 km/h) or Mach 1·14 at sea level, 1,450 mph (2 335 km/h) or Mach 2·2 at 39,370 ft (12 000 m); max. low-altitude penetration speed with typical external ordnance load, 690 mph (1 110 km/h) or Mach 0·9; time to 50,000 ft (15 250 m) at Mach 1·8, 4 min; max. initial climb, 40,160 ft/min (204 m/sec).

Weights: Loaded (clean), 21,384 lb (9 700 kg); max. take-off, 30,864 lb (14 000 kg).

Armament: Two 30-mm DEFA cannon with 125 rpg and seven external ordnance stations. Maximum external load (ordnance and fuel), 9,260 lb (4 200 kg).

Status: Prototype flown May 29, 1970. Series production aircraft available from 1972.

Notes: The Milan (Kite) is a derivative of the Mirage 5 (see pages 74–75) from which it differs primarily in having a more powerful turbojet, a controllable canard, or foreplane, which improves take-off and landing performance, and subsonic manoeuvrability, and a navigational-attack system similar to that of the Jaguar.

DASSAULT MILAN S

Dimensions: Span, 26 ft $11\frac{1}{2}$ in (8,22 m); length, 49 ft $3\frac{1}{2}$ in (15,03 m); height, 13 ft $11\frac{1}{2}$ in (4,25 m); wing area, 375·12 sq ft (34,85 m²).

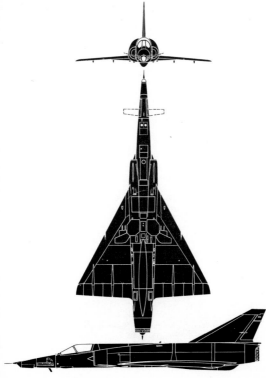

DASSAULT MIRAGE 5

Country of Origin: France.

Type: Single-seat ground attack fighter.

Power Plant: One 9,436 lb (4 280 kg) dry and 13,670 lb (6 200 kg) reheat SNECMA Atar 9C turbojet.

Performance: Max. speed (clean), 835 mph (1 335 km/h) or Mach 1·1 at sea level, 1,386 mph (2 230 km/h) or Mach 2·1 at 39,370 ft (12 000 m); cruise, 594 mph (956 km/h) at 36,090 ft (11 000 m); combat radius with 2,000-lb (907-kg) bomb load (hi-lo-hi profile), 805 mls (1 300 km), (lo-lo-lo profile), 400 mls (650 km); ferry range with max. external fuel, 2,485 mls (4 000 km); time to 36,090 ft (11 000 m) at Mach 0·9, 3 min, to 49,210 ft (15 000 m) at Mach 1·8, 6 min 50 sec.

Weights: Empty equipped, 14,550 lb (6 600 kg); max. loaded, 29,760 lb (13 500 kg).

Armament: Two 30-mm DEFA 5-52 cannon with 125 rpg and seven external ordnance stations. Maximum external load (ordnance and fuel), 9,260 lb (4 200 kg).

Status: Prototype flown May 19, 1967, and first deliveries (to Peru) following May 1968. Assembly (for Belgian Air Force) being undertaken in Belgium by SABCA.

Notes: The Mirage 5 is an export version of the Mirage IIIE (see 1967 edition) optimised for the ground attack role and featuring simplified avionics. Orders at beginning of 1971 included 30 for Pakistan, 16 for Peru (including two two-seaters), 14 for Colombia (plus four two-seat Mirage IIIs), and 106 for Belgium (including 16 two-seaters and 63 for tac-recce role).

DASSAULT MIRAGE 5

Dimensions: Span, 26 ft 11½ in (8,22 m); length, 51 ft 0¼ in (15,55 m); height, 13 ft 11½ in (4,25 m); wing area, 375·12 sq ft (34,85 m²).

DASSAULT MIRAGE F1

Country of Origin: France.

Type: Single-seat multi-purpose fighter.

Power Plant: One 11,023 lb (5 000 kg) dry and 15,873 lb (7 200 kg) reheat SNECMA Atar 9K-50 turbojet.

Performance: Max. speed (clean), 915 mph (1 472 km/h) or Mach 1·2 at sea level, 1,450 mph (2 335 km/h) or Mach 2·2 at 39,370 ft (12 000 m); range cruise, 550 mph (885 km/h) at 29,530 ft (9 000 m); range with max. external fuel, 2,050 mls (3 300 km), with max. external combat load of 8,818 lb (4 000 kg), 560 mls (900 km), with external combat load of 4,410 lb (2 000 kg), 1,430 mls (2 300 km); service ceiling, 65,600 ft (20 000 m).

Weights: Empty, 16,314 lb (7 400 kg); loaded (clean), 24,030 lb (10 900 kg); max. take-off, 32,850 lb (14 900 kg).

Armament: Two 30-mm DEFA cannon and (intercept) 1-3 Matra 530 and two AIM-9 Sidewinder AAMs, or (attack) eight 882-lb (400-kg) bombs, six 66 imp gal (300 l) napalm tanks, five 18-rocket pods, or mix of bombs and missiles, the latter including the AS.30 and AS.37 Martel ASMs.

Status: First of three prototypes flown December 23, 1966. Eighty-five ordered for *Armée de l'Air* by beginning of 1971 with deliveries scheduled for 1972.

Notes: Initial model for *Armée de l'Air* intended primarily for high-altitude intercept role. Proposed versions include F1A for day ground attack role, the F1B two-seat trainer, the F1C interceptor, the F1E multi-role version, and the F1R reconnaissance model.

DASSAULT MIRAGE F1

Dimensions: Span, 27 ft 6¾ in (8,40 m); length, 49 ft 2½ in (15,00 m); height, 14 ft 9 in (4,50 m); wing area, 269·098 sq ft (25 m²).

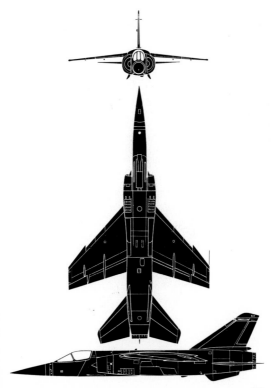

DASSAULT MIRAGE G

Country of Origin: France.

Type: Experimental two-seat multi-purpose fighter.

Power Plant: One 11,684 lb (5 300 kg) dry and 20,503 lb (9 300 kg) reheat SNECMA TF-306E turbofan.

Performance: Max. speed (clean), 990 mph (1 590 km/h) or Mach 1·3 at sea level, 1,650 mph (2 655 km/h) or Mach 2·5 at 41,000 ft (12 500 m); estimated range on internal fuel, 1,865 mls (3 000 km), with three 264 Imp gal (1 200 l) auxiliary tanks, 2,795 mls (4 500 km); service ceiling, 65,620 ft (20 000 m).

Weights: (Estimated) Empty, 22,045 lb (10 000 kg); loaded (clean), 28,660 lb (13 000 kg); max. take-off, 35,275 lb (16 000 kg).

Status: Single-engined Mirage G1 prototype flown October 1967, and two further prototypes (of the twin-engined Mirage G4) ordered late 1968. Financial considerations led, in mid-1970, to programme modifications, and one of the two prototypes initiated as G4 models will now be completed in simplified single-seat form as the Mirage G8, this being scheduled to fly spring 1971 and serve as development aircraft for definitive model for *Armée de l'Air* service by 1980.

Notes: The Mirage G8 differs from the G1 (to which specification and illustrations apply) in being a single-seater powered by two 15,873 lb (7 200 kg) reheat Atar 9K-50 turbojets, operational take-off weight being of the order of 39,685 lb (18 000 kg). It is anticipated that derivatives will have either one or two Super Atar M53 engines with reheat ratings of 18,740–19,840 lb (8 500–9 000 kg).

DASSAULT MIRAGE G

Dimensions: Span (max.), 42 ft 8 in (13,00 m), (min.),
22 ft 11½ in (7,00 m); length, 55 ft 1 in (16,80 m); height,
17 ft 6½ in (5,35 m).

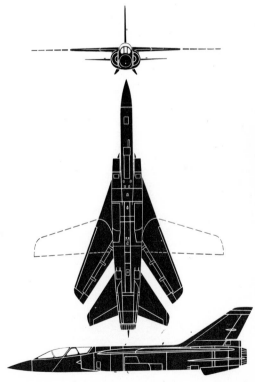

DE HAVILLAND CANADA DHC-5 BUFFALO

Country of Origin: Canada.
Type: STOL military utility transport.
Power Plant: Two 3,055 eshp General Electric CT64-820-1 turboprops.
Performance: Max. cruise, 282 mph (454 km/h) at 10,000 ft (3 050 m); cruise at 80% power, 253 mph (407 km/h), at 52% power, 208 mph (335 km/h); range with 14,100-lb (6 395-kg) payload, 518 mls (834 km), with 8,000-lb (3 629-kg) payload, 1,600 mls (2 575 km), with zero payload, 2,220 mls (3 572 kg); initial climb, 2,080 ft/min (10,56 m/sec); service ceiling, 31,500 ft (9 600 m).
Weights: Operational empty, 22,900 lb (10 387 kg); design take-off, 41,000 lb (18 597 kg); max. overload, 45,100 lb (20 457 kg).
Accommodation: Flight crew of three and 41 troops, 35 paratroops, or 24 casualty stretchers and six medical attendants or seated casualties.
Status: First of four evaluation aircraft (C-8A) for US Army flown April 9, 1964. Deliveries against initial order for 15 (CC-115) for Canadian Armed Forces commenced 1967, 24 delivered to Brazilian Air Force 1969–70, and delivery of 16 for Peruvian Air Force in process 1971.
Notes: Development costs shared equally between the US Army, the Canadian Government and de Havilland Canada. Three survivors of four originally delivered to US Army transferred in 1967 to NASA for research purposes.

DE HAVILLAND CANADA DHC-5 BUFFALO

Dimensions: Span, 99 ft 0 in (29,26 m); length, 79 ft 0 in (24,08 m); height, 28 ft 8 in (8,73 m); wing area, 945 sq ft (87,8 m²).

DE HAVILLAND CANADA DHC-6
TWIN OTTER SERIES 300

Country of Origin: Canada.
Type: STOL utility transport and feederliner.
Power Plant: Two 652 eshp Pratt & Whitney PT6A-27 turboprops.
Performance: Max. cruise, 210 mph (338 km/h) at 10,000 ft (3 050 m); range at max. cruise with 3,250-lb (1 474-kg) payload, 745 mls (1 198 km), with 14 passengers and 45 min reserves, 780 mls (1 255 km); initial climb at 12,500 lb (5 670 kg), 1,600 ft/min (8,1 m/sec); service ceiling, 26,700 ft (8 138 m).
Weights: Basic operational (including pilot), 7,000 lb (3 180 kg); max. take-off, 12,500 lb (5 670 kg).
Accommodation: Flight crew of one or two and accommodation for up to 20 passengers in basic commuter arrangement. Optional commuter layouts for 18 or 19 passengers, and 13–20-passenger utility version.
Status: First of five (Series 100) pre-production aircraft flown May 20, 1965. Series 100 superseded by Series 200 (see 1969 edition) in April 1968, the latter being joined by the Series 300 with the 231st aircraft off the assembly line, deliveries of this version commencing spring 1969. More than 300 of all models delivered by beginning of 1971.
Notes: Series 100 and 200 Twin Otters have 579 eshp PT6A-20s, and the Twin Otter is available as a floatplane.

DHC-6 TWIN OTTER SERIES 300

Dimensions: Span, 65 ft 0 in (19,81 m); length, 51 ft 9 in (15,77 m); height, 18 ft 7 in (5,66 m); wing area, 420 sq ft (39,02 m²).

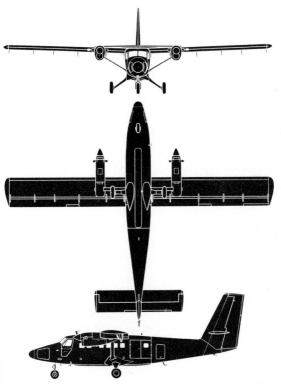

DORNIER DO 28D-2 SKYSERVANT

Country of Origin: Federal Germany.

Type: Light STOL utility aircraft.

Power Plant: Two 380 hp Lycoming IGSO-540-A1E six-cylinder horizontally-opposed engines.

Performance: Max. speed, 199 mph (320 km/h) at 10,000 ft (3 050 m); max. cruise at 75% power, 178 mph (286 km/h) at 10,000 ft (3 050 m); econ. cruise, 143 mph (230 km/h); range with max. fuel and without reserves at econ. cruise, 1,143 mls (1 837 km); initial climb, 1,180 ft/min (6 m/sec); service ceiling, 24,280 ft (7 400 m).

Weights: Empty, 4,775 lb (2 166 kg); max. take-off, 8,050 lb (3 650 kg).

Accommodation: Flight crew of one or two, and 12 passengers in individual seats in main cabin, 13 passengers in inward-facing folding seats, or (ambulance role) five casualty stretchers and five seats for medical attendants or sitting casualties.

Status: First of three prototype Do 28Ds flown February 23, 1966, with production deliveries commencing summer 1967. Production rate of six–eight per month at beginning of 1971.

Notes: Total of 125 Do 28Ds in process of delivery to *Luftwaffe* (105) and *Marineflieger* (20), four of those for the former service are used by the VIP transport unit, the *Flugbereitschaft*, one of these being illustrated above.

84

DORNIER DO 28D-2 SKYSERVANT

Dimensions: Span, 50 ft 10¾ in (15,50 m); length, 37 ft 4¾ in (11,40 m); height, 12 ft 9½ in (3,90 m); wing area, 308 sq ft (28,6 m²).

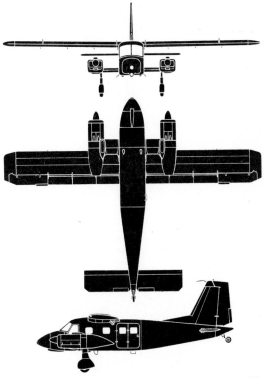

EMBRAER IPD-6504 BANDEIRANTE

Country of Origin: Brazil.
Type: Light military general-purpose transport.
Power Plant: Two 680 shp Pratt & Whitney PT6A-27 turboprops.
Performance: Max. speed, 285 mph (458 km/h) at 9,840 ft (3 000 m); max. cruise, 267 mph (430 km/h) at 8,300 ft (2 530 m); max. range with 30 min reserves, 1,240 mls (2 000 km) at 10,000 ft (3 280 m); initial climb, 1,870 ft/min (9,5 m/sec); service ceiling, 25,000 ft (7 600 m).
Weights: Max. take-off, 10,692 lb (4 850 kg).
Accommodation: Normal flight crew of two and up to 12 passengers in individual seats or four casualty stretchers and two medical attendants.
Status: First of four prototypes flown October 26, 1968, and production of initial series of 20 aircraft scheduled to commence during 1971, this being followed by a further series of 80, deliveries being expected to attain two per month during 1972.
Notes: Developed by a division of the Centro Técnico de Aeronáutica, the Bandeirante is being manufactured by the Emprêsa Brasileira de Aeronautica SA (Embraer) primarily for the Brazilian Air Force which has a requirement for 80 Bandeirantes for transport, aero-medical and navigational training tasks. The production model (to which the specification refers) will differ in minor details to the prototypes (the third example of which is illustrated) which are powered by 550 shp PT6A-20 turboprops.

EMBRAER IPD-6504 BANDEIRANTE

Dimensions: Span, 50 ft $2\frac{1}{4}$ in (15,30 m); length, 44 ft $3\frac{1}{2}$ in (13,50 m); height, 17 ft $8\frac{3}{4}$ in (5,40 m); wing area, 312·153 sq ft (29 m²).

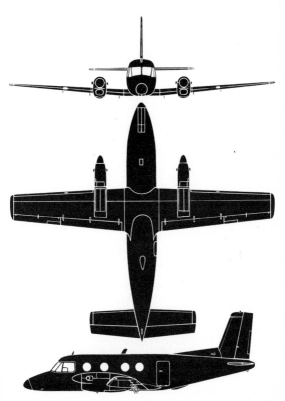

EMBRAER IPD-6901 IPANEMA

Country of Origin: Brazil.

Type: Single-seat agricultural aircraft.

Power Plant: One 260 hp Lycoming O-540-H1A5 six-cylinder horizontally-opposed engine.

Performance: (With agricultural equipment) Max. speed, 123 mph (198 km/h) at sea level; max. cruise, 107 mph (173 km/h); econ. cruise, 103 mph (165 km/h); range with max. payload, 360 mls (580 km), with max. fuel and without agricultural equipment, 745 mls (1 200 km) at 110 mph (177 km/h); initial climb, 951 ft/min (15,3 m/sec); service ceiling, 12,960 ft (3 950 m).

Weights: Empty equipped, 1,433 lb (650 kg); max. take-off, 3,086 lb (1 400 kg).

Status: First prototype flown July 30, 1970, and production scheduled to commence in 1971 with initial series of 50 aircraft of which 10 have been ordered by the Ministry of Agriculture.

Notes: Development of the Ipanema to meet a Brazilian Ministry of Agriculture specification was initiated by a division of the Centro Técnico de Aeronautica, development responsibility being transferred to Embraer in January 1970. Standard agricultural equipment comprises a 1,212-lb (550-kg) container suitable for dust or liquid. Spray booms project aft and below the wing trailing edges. Series production will be undertaken in collaboration with the Sociedade Aerotec Limitada.

EMBRAER IPD-6901 IPANEMA

Dimensions: Span, 36 ft 9 in (11,20 m); length, 24 ft 4$\frac{1}{2}$ in (7,43 m); height, 7 ft 2$\frac{1}{2}$ in (2,20 m); wing area, 193·75 sq ft (18 m²).

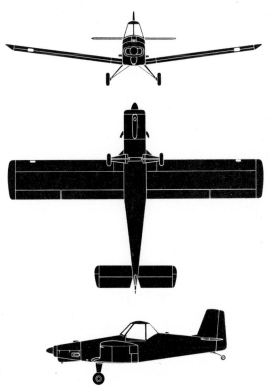

FIAT G.91Y

Country of Origin: Italy.

Type: Single-seat light tactical fighter-bomber and reconnaissance aircraft.

Power Plant: Two 2,725 lb (1 236 kg) dry and 4,080 lb (1 850 kg) reheat General Electric J85-GE-13A turbojets.

Performance: Max. speed, 690 mph (1 110 km/h) or Mach 0·9 at sea level, 670 mph (1 080 km/h) or Mach 0·95 at 32,810 ft (10 000 m); range cruise at 490 ft (150 m), 390 mph (630 km/h); typical tactical radius for lo-lo-lo mission with 2,910-lb (1 320-kg) payload, 240 mls (385 km); ferry range with two 176 Imp gal (800 l) auxiliary tanks and 10% reserves, 2,110 mls (3 400 km); max. initial climb, 17,000 ft/min (86,36 m/sec); service ceiling, 41,000 ft (12 500 m).

Weights: Empty, 8,598 lb (3 900 kg); normal max. take-off, 17,196 lb (7 800 kg); max. overload take-off, 19,180 lb (8 700 kg).

Armament: Two 30-mm DEFA 552 cannon. Four underwing stores stations for max. of 4,000 lb (1 814 kg) ordnance.

Status: First of two prototypes flown December 27, 1966, and first of 20 pre-production aircraft flown July 1968. Delivery of 55 production aircraft to Italian Air Force in process at beginning of 1971.

Notes: Prototype of a modified version with more advanced avionics (including Saab bombing computer) for evaluation by Switzerland was flown on October 16, 1970.

FIAT G.91Y

Dimensions: Span, 29 ft 6½ in (9,01 m); length, 38 ft 3½ in (11,67 m); height, 14 ft 6⅓ in (4,43 m); wing area, 195·149 sq ft (18,13 m²).

FIAT G.222

Country of Origin: Italy.

Type: General-purpose military transport.

Power Plant: Two 2,970 shp General Electric CT64-820 turboprops. (Proposed) Two 3,400 shp T64-P4D turboprops.

Performance: (Estimated with T64-P4D engines) Max. speed, 329 mph (530 km/h) at sea level; normal cruise, 273 mph (440 km/h) at 14,750 ft (4 500 m); range with 11,025-lb (5 000-kg) payload, 1,920 mls (3 250 km), with max. fuel, 3,262 mls (5 250 km); max. initial climb rate, 1,890 ft/min (9,6 m/sec).

Weights: Empty, 29,320 lb (13 300 kg); empty equipped, 32,408 lb (14 700 kg); max. take-off, 57,320 lb (26 000 kg).

Accommodation: Flight crew of three or four and seats for 44 fully-equipped troops or 40 paratroops. Alternative loads include 36 casualty stretchers, two jeep-type vehicles or equivalent freight.

Status: First of two prototypes flown July 18, 1970. Programme currently limited to two flying prototypes and static test airframe, and decision concerning future production likely to be delayed until completion of prototypes' trials in 1971.

Notes: Prototypes powered by CT64-820 turboprops and unpressurised, but the proposed production model will have uprated T64-P4D turboprops and provision for pressurisation. The G.222 is being proposed as a successor to some of the Italian Air Force's ageing Fairchild C-119 transports.

FIAT G.222

Dimensions: Span, 94 ft 5¾ in (28,80 m); length, 74 ft 5½ in (22,70 m); height, 32 ft 1¾ in (9,80 m); wing area, 970·9 sq ft (90,2 m²).

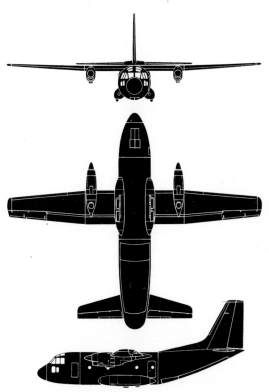

FMA IA 58 PUCARÁ

Country of Origin: Argentina.
Type: Tandem two-seat counter-insurgency aircraft.
Power Plant: Two 904 ehp Garrett AiResearch TPE-331-U-303 turboprops.
Performance: Max. speed, 308 mph (495 km/h) at 9,840 ft (3 000 m); max. cruise, 295 mph (475 km/h) at 9,840 ft (3 000 m); econ. cruise, 257 mph (414 km/h); range with max. fuel, 2,235 mls (3 600 km); initial climb, 2,955 ft/min (15 m/sec); service ceiling at 11,464 lb (5 200 kg), 29,200 ft (8 900 m).
Weights: Empty equipped, 7,826 lb (3 550 kg); max. take-off, 13,668 lb (6 200 kg).
Armament: Two 20-mm Hispano cannon and four 7,62-mm FN machine guns. Hard points beneath fuselage and outer wing panels for various combinations of bombs, missiles or weapons pods.
Status: First prototype (illustrated) flown on August 20, 1969, and first of two Astazou-powered prototypes flown during 1970. Argentine Air Force requirement for 80 production examples, and construction of initial batch of 50 tentatively authorised with deliveries commencing 1972.
Notes: First prototype reportedly underpowered and definitive acceptance trials being conducted during 1971 with second prototype powered by 1,022 eshp Turboméca Astazou XVIG turboprops.

FMA IA 58 PUCARÁ

Dimensions: Span. 47 ft $6\frac{3}{4}$ in (14,50 m); length, 45 ft $7\frac{1}{4}$ in (13,90 m); height, 17 ft $2\frac{1}{4}$ in (5,24 m); wing area, 326·1 sq ft (30,3 m²).

FOKKER F.27 FRIENDSHIP SRS. 500

Country of Origin: Netherlands.
Type: Short- to medium-range commercial transport.
Power Plant: Two 2,250 eshp Rolls-Royce Dart 532-7 turboprops.
Performance: Max. cruise, 322 mph (518 km/h) at 20,000 ft (6 095 m); normal cruise at 38,000 lb (17 237 kg), 292 mph (470 km/h) at 20,000 ft (6 095 m); range with max. payload, 667 mls (1 075 km), with max. fuel and 9,680-lb (4 390-kg) payload, 1,099 mls (1 805 km); initial climb at max. take-off weight, 1,200 ft/min (6,1 m/sec); service ceiling at 38,000 lb (17 237 kg), 28,500 ft (8 690 m).
Weights: Empty, 25,300 lb (11 475 kg); operational empty, 26,190 lb (11 879 kg); max. take-off, 45,000 lb (20 411 kg).
Accommodation: Basic flight crew of two or three and standard seating for 52 passengers. Alternative arrangements for up to 56 passengers.
Status: First Srs. 500 flown November 15, 1967. Production currently standardising on Srs. 500 and 600. Orders for the Friendship (including those licence-built in the USA by Fairchild Hiller) totalled 568 by beginning of 1971.
Notes: By comparison with basic Srs. 200 (see 1968 edition), the Srs. 500 has a 4 ft 11 in (1,5 m) fuselage stretch. The Srs. 400 "Combiplane" (see 1966 edition) and the equivalent military Srs. 400M are convertible cargo or combined cargo-passenger versions of the Srs. 200, and the current Srs. 600 is similar to the Srs. 400 but lacks the reinforced and watertight cargo floor.

FOKKER F.27 FRIENDSHIP SRS. 500

Dimensions: Span, 95 ft 1¾ in (29,00 m); length, 82 ft 2½ in (25,06 m); height, 28 ft 7¼ in (8,71 m); wing area, 753·47 sq ft (70 m²).

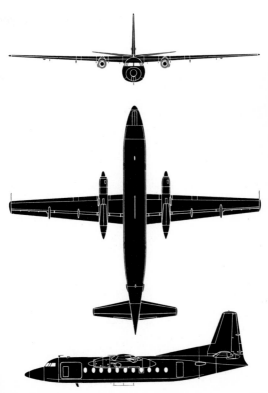

FOKKER F.28 FELLOWSHIP MK. 1000

Country of Origin: Netherlands.

Type: Short-range commercial transport.

Power Plant: Two 9,850 lb (4 468 kg) Rolls-Royce RB.183-2 Spey Mk. 555-15 turbofans.

Performance: Max. cruise, 528 mph (849 km/h) at 21,000 ft (6 400 m); long-range cruise, 427 mph (687 km/h) at 30,000 ft (9 150 m); range with 60 passengers, 1,266 mls (2 038 km), with max. standard fuel, 1,336 mls (2 149 km); max. cruise altitude, 30,000 ft (9 150 m).

Weights: Empty, 31,263 lb (14 180 kg); operational empty, 34,500 lb (15 650 kg); max. take-off, 63,000 lb (28 580 kg).

Accommodation: Normal flight crew of two and 40 passengers in four-abreast seating or 60–65 passengers in five-abreast seating.

Status: First prototype Fellowship flown on May 9, 1967, followed by first production aircraft on May 21, 1968. First customer delivery (to LTU) on February 24, 1969. Production rate of two per month scheduled for 1971. Orders for the Fellowship totalled 38 aircraft by the beginning of 1971 with 23 delivered.

Notes: A stretched version of the F.28, the Fellowship Mk. 2000 incorporating additional fuselage sections increasing overall length to 97 ft 1¾ in (29,61 m), was scheduled to commence its flight test programme early in 1971. The lengthened fuselage permits an increase in accommodation providing for up to 79 passengers in an all-tourist configuration. The F.28 is a European co-operative effort with components built by VFW and MBB in Germany and Short Brothers in the UK.

FOKKER F.28 FELLOWSHIP MK. 1000

Dimensions: Span, 77 ft $4\frac{1}{4}$ in (23,58 m); length, 89 ft $10\frac{3}{4}$ in (27,40 m); height, 27 ft $9\frac{1}{2}$ in (8,47 m); wing area, 822 sq ft (76,4 m²).

GATES LEARJET 24D

Country of Origin: USA.

Type: Light business executive transport.

Power Plant: Two 2,950 lb (1 340 kg) General Electric CJ610-6 turbojets.

Performance: Max. speed, 545 mph (877 km/h) at 31,000 ft (9 450 m); max. cruise, 534 mph (859 km/h) at 45,000 ft (13 720 m); econ. cruise, 481 mph (774 km/h) at 45,000 ft (13 720 m); range with max. fuel and 45 min reserves, 1,960 mls (3 154 km); initial climb, 6,300 ft/min (32 m/sec); service ceiling, 45,000 ft (13 720 m).

Weights: Empty equipped, 6,851 lb (3 107 kg); max. take-off, 13,500 lb (6 124 kg).

Accommodation: Normal flight crew of two, and up to six passengers in main cabin.

Status: The prototype Learjet was flown on October 7, 1963, the initial production model being the Learjet 23 (see 1966 edition) of which deliveries began in October 1964. After delivery of 104 Learjet 23s this model was superseded by the Learjet 24, deliveries commencing in March 1966. This was succeeded by the Model 24B late 1968, this giving place in turn to the current Learjet 24D of which deliveries began during the summer of 1970. Some 300 Learjets of all versions had been delivered by January 1971.

Notes: Learjet 24D is one of three current models, the others being two versions of the stretched (by 4 ft 2 in/1,27 m) Learjet 25 (see 1967 edition), the 25B, with similar refinements to the 24D, and the longer-range 23C'. The proposed lower-cost, lighter Learjet 24C has been abandoned.

GATES LEARJET 24D

Dimensions: Span, 35 ft 7 in (10,84 m); length, 43 ft 3 in (13,18 m); height, 12 ft 7 in (3,84 m); wing area, 231·77 sq ft (21,53 m²).

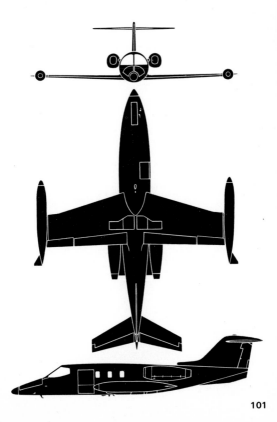

GENERAL DYNAMICS F-111E

Country of Origin: USA.

Type: Two-seat tactical strike fighter.

Power Plant: Two 19,600 lb (8 890 kg) reheat Pratt & Whitney TF30-P-9 turbofans.

Performance: Max. speed, 865 mph (1 390 km/h) or Mach 1·2 at sea level, 1,650 mph (2 655 km/h) or Mach 2·5 at 40,000 ft (12 190 m); ferry range with max. internal fuel, 3,800 mls (6 115 km); tactical radius with 16,000-lb (7 257-kg) combat load for hi-lo-hi mission profile, 1,500 mls (2 415 km); approx. max. climb at 74,000 lb (33 566 kg), 40,000 ft/min (203,2 m/sec).

Weights: Empty operational, 47,500 lb (23 525 kg); normal take-off, 74,000 lb (33 566 kg); max. overload take-off, 91,500 lb (41 504 kg).

Armament: One 20-mm M-61A1 rotary cannon with 2,000 rounds or two 750-lb M117 bombs internally. Approx. max. ordnance load of 30,000 lb (13 608 kg) for short-range interdiction. External ordnance carried by four 4,000-lb (1 814-kg) capacity swivelling wing stations and four fixed wing stations of similar capacity.

Status: First of 28 test and development F-111s flown December 21, 1964. Initial production model, the F-111A (see 1969 edition), of which 141 built. Superseded by F-111E (94 aircraft) from late 1969, these being followed by F-111D (96 aircraft) and F-111F (82 aircraft), with production phase-out late 1972.

Notes: F-111E differs from F-111A in having revised air intake geometry and TF30-P-9 turbofans, and the similarly-powered F-111D features more advanced avionics. The F-111F is to have uprated TF30-P-100 series engines and a simplified avionics system.

GENERAL DYNAMICS F-111E

Dimensions: Span (max.), 63 ft 0 in (19,20 m), (min.),
31 ft 11⅓ in (9,74); length, 73 ft 6 in (22,40 m); height,
17 ft 1⅓ in (5,22 m).

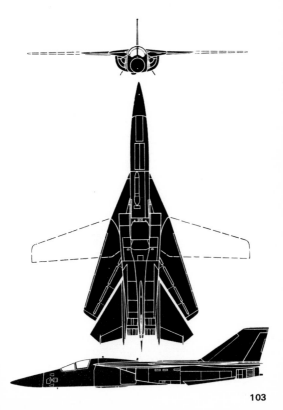

GENERAL DYNAMICS FB-111A

Country of Origin: USA.

Type: Two-seat strategic bomber.

Power Plant: Two 20,500 lb (9 295 kg) reheat Pratt & Whitney TF30-P-7 turbofans.

Performance: Max. speed in clean configuration, 838 mph (1 350 km/h) or Mach 1·1 at sea level, 1,450 mph (2 334 km/h) or Mach 2·2 at 40,000 ft (12 190 m); tactical radius with subsonic cruise to target, supersonic approach and escape, and return at subsonic cruise, carrying four SRAM to target, 1,200 mls (1 930 km); ferry range with four 500 Imp gal (2 273 l) external tanks, 4,100 mls (6 600 km); service ceiling, 65,000 ft (19 810 m).

Weights: (Estimated) Max. take-off, 100,000 lb (45 360 kg).

Armament: Up to six 2,200-lb (998-kg) Boeing AGM-69A short-range attack missiles (SRAM) on external pylons, or conventional ordnance loads up to 37,500 lb (16 010 kg). Typical short-range interdiction load comprises 50 750-lb (340-kg) bombs on multiple ejection racks.

Status: First FB-111A flown July 13, 1968, first delivery to USAF following October 8, 1969. Current order calls for 76 aircraft for early-1971 completion.

Notes: The FB-111A airframe is essentially similar to that of the F-111E (see pages 102–103), but employs the long-span wings originally developed for the F-111B (see 1966 edition) and a new undercarriage.

GENERAL DYNAMICS FB-111A

Dimensions: Span (max.), 70 ft 0 in (21,34 m), (min.), 33 ft 11 in (10,34 m); length, 73 ft 6 in (22,40 m); height, 17 ft 1½ in (5,22 m).

GRUMMAN A-6 INTRUDER

Country of Origin: USA.

Type: Two-seat shipboard low-level strike aircraft.

Power Plant: Two 9,300 lb (4 218 kg) Pratt & Whitney J52-P-8A turbojets.

Performance: Max. speed at 36,655 lb (16 626 kg) in clean condition, 685 mph (1 102 km/h) or Mach 0·9 at sea level, 625 mph (1 006 km/h) or Mach 0·94 at 36,000 ft (10 970 m); average cruise, 480 mph (772 km/h) at 32,750–43,800 ft (9 980–13 350 m); range with max. internal fuel and four Bullpup ASMs, 1,920 mls (3 090 km), with single store and four 250 Imp gal (1 136 l) external tanks, 3,040 mls (4 890 km).

Weights: Empty, 25,684 lb (11 650 kg); loaded (clean), 37,116 lb (16 836 kg); max. overload take-off, 60,280 lb (27 343 kg).

Armament: Max. external ordnance load of 15,000 lb (6 804 kg) distributed between five 3,600-lb (1 633-kg) stores stations.

Status: First of eight test and development aircraft flown April 19, 1960 and first delivery to US Navy (A-6A) on February 7, 1963.

Notes: Specification relates to basic A-6A (see 1970 edition), drawing depicts A-6B which differs in having equipment for AGM-78A Standard ARM (Anti-Radiation Missile), and photo illustrates the A-6C which has a detachable ventral turret for low-light television and infrared sensors. The KA-6D is a shipboard tanker version, and the A-6E has more advanced avionics and flew in prototype form on February 27, 1970. The EA-6A and EA-6B (see 1969 edition) are two- and four-seat electronic countermeasures versions respectively.

GRUMMAN A-6 INTRUDER

Dimensions: Span, 53 ft 0 in (16,15 m); length, 54 ft 7 in (16,64 m); height, 15 ft 7 in (4,75 m); wing area, 529 sq ft (49,15 m²).

GRUMMAN F-14A TOMCAT

Country of Origin: USA.

Type: Two-seat shipboard multi-purpose fighter.

Power Plant: Two (approx) 22,500 lb (10 205 kg) reheat Pratt & Whitney TF30-P-412 turbofans.

Performance: (Estimated) Max. speed with four AIM-7 Sparrow missiles for intercept mission at approx. 53,000 lb (24 040 kg), 910 mph (1 470 km/h) or Mach 1·2 at sea level, 1,650 mph (2 655 km/h) or Mach 2·5 at 40,000 ft (12 190 m).

Weights: (Estimated) Empty, 36,000 lb (16 330 kg); normal take-off (intercept mission), 53,000 lb (24 040 kg).

Armament: One 20-mm M-61A1 rotary cannon and (intercept mission) six AIM-7 Sparrow AAMs or six AIM-54 Phoenix and four AIM-9 Sidewinder AAMs.

Status: First of 12 research and development aircraft commenced flight trials on December 21, 1970, with second scheduled to fly March 1971. Initial quantity of 26 production F-14As ordered by January 1971 when production was scheduled to attain one per month, increasing to two per month in July 1972. US Navy has option on 463 F-14 series fighters.

Notes: F-14A is scheduled to attain operational status early in 1973, the 68th and subsequent aircraft being completed to F-14B standard with advanced technology Pratt & Whitney F401-PW-401 turbofans of some 30,000 lb (13 610) kg), increasing thrust/weight ratio from 0·84 to 1·16, estimated acceleration from Mach 0·8 to Mach 1·8 being 1·27 minutes. The F-14B will commence fleet indoctrination late 1973 or early 1974. The proposed F-14C version of the Tomcat will embody a more advanced avionics system.

GRUMMAN F-14A TOMCAT

Dimensions: Span (max.), 64 ft 1½ in (19,54 m), (min.), 33 ft 2½ in (10,12 m); length, 61 ft 10½ in (18,86 m); height, 16 ft 0 in (4,88 m).

HAL HF-24 MARUT MK. 1T

Country of Origin: India.

Type: Two-seat operational conversion trainer.

Power Plant: Two 4,850 lb (2 200 kg) HAL-built Rolls-Royce Bristol Orpheus 703 turbojets.

Performance: Max. speed, 705 mph (1 135 km/h) or Mach 0·925 at sea level, 675 mph (1 086 km/h) or Mach 1·02 at 40,000 ft (12 200 m); tactical radius (internal fuel) at 560 mph (900 km/h) or Mach 0·85 at 36,000 ft (10 970 m); time to 40,000 ft (12 190 m), 7 min; service ceiling, 46,000 ft (14 020 m).

Weights: (Mk. 1A) Empty, 13,658 lb (6 195 kg); loaded (clean), 19,734 lb (8 951 kg); max. overload take-off, 24,250 lb (11 000 kg).

Armament: Four 30-mm Aden cannon and 48 air-to-air rockets. Four 1,000-lb (453,5-kg) capacity underwing stores stations.

Status: Prototype HF-24T flown April 30, 1970. Delivery of initial batch of 10 to commence late 1971. Total Indian Air Force requirement for the two-seat Marut reportedly numbers 75–85 aircraft.

Notes: The Marut (Wind Spirit) Mk. 1T is a tandem two-seat development of the Marut Mk. 1A (see 1966 edition) ground attack fighter currently serving with Nos. 10 and 210 Squadrons of the Indian Air Force. The Mk. 1T, a conversion of the 46th production Marut airframe, retains full operational capability. Current production orders call for 100 Mk. 1As, and two airframes have been fitted with 6,000-lb (2 720-kg) reheat versions of the Orpheus 703 as prototypes of the Marut Mk. 1R. At the beginning of 1971 consideration was being given to matching the Marut airframe with the Rolls-Royce Turboméca Adour for Mach 2·0 performance.

110

HAL HF-24 MARUT MK. 1T

Dimensions: Span, 29 ft 6¼ in (9,00 m); length, 52 ft 0¾ in (15,87 m); height, 11 ft 9¾ in (3,60 m); wing area, 273·9 sq ft (25,45 m²).

HAWKER SIDDELEY 125-600

Country of Origin: United Kingdom.

Type: Light business executive transport.

Power Plant: Two 3,750 lb (1 701 kg) Rolls-Royce Viper 601 turbojets.

Performance: (Estimated) Max. cruise, 510 mph (820 km/h) at 31,000 ft (9 450 m); econ. cruise, 450 mph (734 km/h) at 38,000 ft (11 580 m); range with max. fuel and reserves for 45 min hold, 1,960 mls (3 154 km); initial climb, 3,600 ft/min (18,3 m/sec); service ceiling, 41,000 ft (12 495 m).

Weights: (Estimated) Empty equipped, 12,500 lb (5 670 kg); max. take-off, 25,000 lb (7 620 kg).

Accommodation: Normal flight crew of two and alternative interior layouts for from six to 14 passengers.

Status: First of two prototype HS 125-600s was scheduled to commence its flight test programme early in 1971 with first customer deliveries anticipated late 1971.

Notes: The HS 125-600, which is to be marketed in North America by Beech Aircraft Corporation as the BH-600, is essentially a higher-powered, stretched version of the HS 125-400 (see 1970 edition), an additional section in the forward fuselage permitting two more passengers to be carried, and the Viper 601s providing more thrust and improved specific fuel consumption.

HAWKER SIDDELEY 125-600

Dimensions: Span, 47 ft 0 in (14,33 m); length, 50 ft 6 in (15,39 m); height, 17 ft 3 in (5,25 m); wing area, 353 sq ft (32,8 m²).

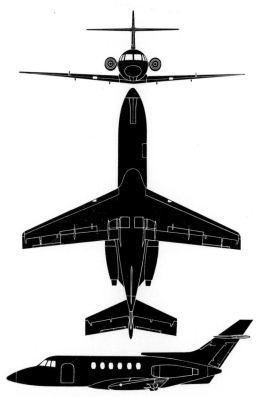

HAWKER SIDDELEY 748 SERIES 2A

Country of Origin: United Kingdom.
Type: Short- to medium-range commercial transport.
Power Plant: Two 2,280 ehp Rolls-Royce Dart R.Da.7 Mk. 532-2L turboprops.
Performance: Max. speed at 40,000 lb (18 145 kg), 312 mph (502 km/h) at 16,000 ft (4 875 m); max. cruise, 287 mph (462 km/h) at 15,000 ft (4 570 m); econ. cruise, 267 mph (430 km/h) at 20,000 ft (6 095 m); range cruise, 259 mph (418 km/h) at 25,000 ft (7 620 m); range with max. fuel and reserves for 45 min hold and 230-mile (370-km) diversion, 1,862 mls (2 996 km), with max. payload and same reserves, 690 mls (1 110 km).
Weights: Basic operational, 25,361 lb (11 504 kg); max. take-off, 44,495 lb (20 182 kg).
Accommodation: Normal flight crew of two and standard cabin arrangement for 40 passengers in paired seats. Alternative high-density arrangement for 58 passengers.
Status: First prototype flown June 24, 1960, and first production model (Srs. 1) on August 30, 1961. Srs. 1 superseded by Srs. 2 in 1962, this being in turn superseded by current Srs. 2A from mid-1967. Total of 245 ordered by beginning of 1971.
Notes: Manufactured under licence in India by HAL for Indian Airlines (24) and Indian Air Force (five Srs. 1 and 22 Srs. 2) at rate of nine per year.

HAWKER SIDDELEY 748 SERIES 2A

Dimensions: Span, 98 ft 6 in (30,02 m); length, 67 ft 0 in (20,42 m); height, 24 ft 10 in (7,57 m); wing area, 810·75 sq ft (75,35 m²).

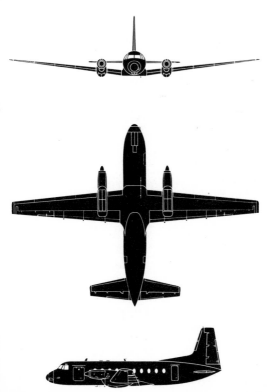

HAWKER SIDDELEY BUCCANEER S.MK.2B

Country of Origin: United Kingdom.
Type: Two-seat strike and reconnaissance aircraft.
Power Plant: Two 11,100 lb (5 035 kg) Rolls-Royce RB. 168-1A Spey Mk. 101 turbofans.
Performance: (Estimated) Max. speed, 645 mph (1 040 km/h) or Mach 0·85 at 250 ft (75 m); 620 mph (998 km/h) or Mach 0·92 at 30,000 ft (9 145 m); typical low-level cruise, 570 mph (917 km/h) or Mach 0·75 at 3,000 ft (915 m); tactical radius for hi-lo-lo-hi mission with standard fuel, 500–600 mls (805–965 km).
Weights: Max. take-off, 59,000 lb (26 762 kg).
Armament: Max. ordnance load of 16,000 lb (7 257 kg), including four 500-lb (227-kg), 540-lb (245-kg), or 1,000-lb (453,5-kg) bombs internally, and up to three 1,000-lb (453,5-kg) or six 500-lb (227-kg) bombs on each of four wing stations.
Status: First S. Mk. 2B for RAF flown January 8, 1970, with 26 built to this standard to be delivered by early 1972. Proportion of 84 S. Mk. 2s built for Royal Navy being modified for RAF use as S. Mk. 2As, and most of these ultimately to be converted to S. Mk. 2Bs.
Notes: The S. Mk. 2A embodies avionic, system, and equipment modifications for RAF service, and wing and weapon-pylon changes to provide Martel missile capability. S. Mk. 2B introduces 425 Imp gal (1 932 l) fuel tank on rotating bomb door (seen on accompanying drawing) and undercarriage changes to accommodate new gross weight of 59,000 lb (26 762 kg).

116

HAWKER SIDDELEY BUCCANEER S. MK. 2B

Dimensions: Span, 44 ft 0 in (13,41 m); length, 63 ft 5 in (19,33 m); height, 16 ft 3 in (4,95 m); wing area, 514·7 sq ft (47,82 m²).

HAWKER SIDDELEY HARRIER G.R. MK. 1

Country of Origin: United Kingdom.

Type: Single-seat V/STOL strike and reconnaissance fighter.

Power Plant: One 19,200 lb (8 710 kg) Rolls-Royce Bristol Pegasus 101 vectored-thrust turbofan.

Performance: Max. speed, 720 mph (1 160 km/h) or Mach 0·95 at 1,000 ft (305 m), with typical external ordnance load, 640–660 mph (1 030–1 060 km) or Mach 0·85–0·87 at 1,000 ft (305 m); max. speed in clean condition at 35,000 ft (10 670 m), 610 mph (980 km/h) or Mach 0·93; tactical radius for hi-lo-hi mission with two 100 Imp gal (455 l) external tanks, 400 mls (644 km); ferry range with two 330 Imp gal (1 500 l) external tanks, 2,250 mls (3 620 km).

Weights: Empty equipped, 13,550 lb (6 146 kg); max. take-off (VTOL), 16,000 lb (7 257 kg); max. take-off (STOL), 21,500 lb (9 752 kg).

Armament: Provision for two 30-mm Aden cannon with 130 rpg and up to 5,000 lb (2 268 kg) of ordnance on five external stores stations.

Status: First of six pre-production aircraft flown August 31, and first production G.R. Mk. 1 following on December 28, 1967. Current orders for RAF call for 77 G.R. Mk. 1s plus 13 two-seat T. Mk. 2s (see 1969 edition). First T. Mk. 2 development aircraft flown April 24, 1969, and first Mk. 50 for the US Marine Corps flown November 20, 1970.

Notes: Export models with 21,500 lb (9 752 kg) Pegasus 103 known as Mk. 50 (single-seat) and Mk. 51 (two-seat). Initial batch of 30 Mk. 50s for US Marine Corps (as AV-8As) for 1971 delivery, first 10 with interim 20,500-lb (9 300-kg) Pegasus 102.

HAWKER SIDDELEY HARRIER G.R. MK. 1

Dimensions: Span, 25 ft 3 in (7,70 m); length, 45 ft 7$\frac{3}{4}$ in (13,91 m); height, 11 ft 3 in (3,43 m); wing area, 201·1 sq ft (18,68 m²).

HAWKER SIDDELEY NIMROD M.R. MK. 1

Country of Origin: United Kingdom.

Type: Long-range maritime patrol aircraft.

Power Plant: Four (approx) 11,500 lb (5 217 kg) Rolls-Royce RB. 168-20 Spey Mk. 250 turbofans.

Performance: (Estimated) Max. cruise, 500–530 mph (805-853 km/h) at 31,000–33,000 ft (9 450–10 060 m); long-range cruise, 460 mph (740 km/h) at 30,000 ft (9 145 m); minimum search speed, 210 mph (338 km/h); loiter endurance on two engines, 12–14 hrs.

Weights: Max. take-off 175,000–178,000 lb (79 380–80 740 kg).

Armament: Ventral weapons bay accommodating full range of ASW weapons (homing torpedoes, mines, depth charges, etc) and two underwing pylons for AS.12 or Martel ASMs.

Accommodation: Normal flight crew of three on flight deck with nine navigators and sensor operators in tactical compartment. Provision is made for conversion for the trooping role and in this configuration up to 45 troops may be accommodated in the rear pressure cabin.

Status: First of two Nimrod prototypes employing modified Comet 4C airframes flown May 23, 1967. First of current batch of 38 production Nimrods flown on June 28, 1968, followed by first delivery to RAF on October 2, 1969. RAF order scheduled for completion mid-1971. These to be followed by three further aircraft for specialised trials purposes.

Notes: The world's first shore-based turbojet-propelled maritime patrol aircraft, the Nimrod employs the basic structure of the Comet 4C transport (see 1963 edition) and will equip five RAF squadrons.

120

HAWKER SIDDELEY NIMROD M.R. MK. 1

Dimensions: Span, 114 ft 10 in (35,00 m); length, 126 ft 9 in (38,63 m); height, 29 ft 8$\frac{1}{2}$ in (9,01 m); wing area, 2,121 sq ft (197,05 m²).

HAWKER SIDDELEY TRIDENT 3B

Country of Origin: United Kingdom.
Type: Short-haul commercial transport.
Power Plant: Three 11,930 lb (5 411 kg) Rolls-Royce RB.163—25 Mk. 512-5W turbofans plus one 5,250 lb (2 381 kg) Rolls-Royce RB.162-86 turbojet.
Performance: Max. cruise, 601 mph (967 km/h) at 28,300 ft (8 625 m); econ. cruise, 533 mph (858 km/h) at 29,000–33,000 ft (8 000–10 000 m); typical high-speed cruise, 580 mph (933 km/h) at 25,000 ft (7 620 m); range with max. payload and reserves for 250 mls (402 km) and 45 min hold, 1,658 mls (2 668 km), with max. payload and same reserves, 1,094 mls (1 760 km).
Weights: Operational empty as 128-seater, 83,473 lb (37 863 kg), as 152-seater, 83,104 lb (37 695 kg); max. take-off, 150,000 lb (68 040 kg).
Accommodation: Basic flight crew of three and alternative arrangements for 14 first-class and 114 tourist-class passengers, or 152 tourist-class passengers. High-density arrangements for 164 or 171 passengers.
Status: First Trident 3B flown December 11, 1969. Twenty-six (with options on 10 more) ordered for BEA, with which airline the Trident 3B was scheduled to enter service early 1971.
Notes: The Trident 3B is a high-capacity short-haul development of the Trident 1E (see 1966 edition) with a stretched fuselage and similar power plants and wing modifications to those of the Trident 2E (see 1969 edition). The 3B also embodies wing area, wing incidence, and flap span increases.

HAWKER SIDDELEY TRIDENT 3B

Dimensions: Span, 98 ft 0 in (29,87 m); length, 131 ft 2 in (39,98 m); height, 28 ft 3 in (8,61 m); wing area, 1,493 sq ft (138,7 m²).

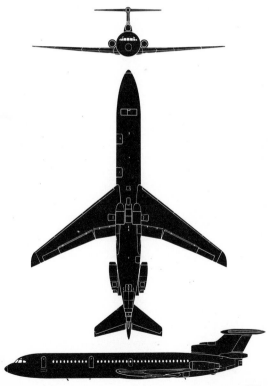

HISPANO HA-220

Country of Origin: Spain.
Type: Single-seat light ground attack aircraft.
Power Plant: Two 1,058 lb (480 kg) Turboméca Marboré VI turbojets.
Performance: Max. speed, 410 mph (660 km/h) or Mach 0·54 at sea level, 430 mph (692 km/h) or Mach 0·63 at 22,965 ft (7 000 m); max. cruise, 340 mph (547 km/h) at sea level, 360 mph (580 km/h) at 19,685 ft (6 000 m); range with max. internal fuel and no reserves, 510 mls (820 km) at sea level, 1,025 mls (1 650 km) at 29,530 ft (9 000 m); service ceiling, 42,650 ft (13 000 m).
Weights: (Estimated) Empty equipped, 4,630 lb (2 100 kg); max. take-off, 7,937 lb (3 600 kg).
Armament: Two 7,7-mm Breda machine guns and various ordnance loads on four 551-lb (250-kg) capacity wing and two 375-lb (170-kg) capacity fuselage stores stations.
Status: First of initial batch of 25 HA-220s ordered for Spanish Air Force flown on April 25, 1970, with completion of order scheduled for mid-1971.
Notes: The HA-220 is a single-seat ground attack derivative of the HA-200E Super Saeta advanced trainer (see 1969 edition) from which it differs primarily in having self-sealing fuel tanks, an additional tank in place of the second seat of the trainer, light armour protection for the cockpit and other areas vulnerable to groundfire, additional stores stations, and appropriate avionics for the ground attack role.

HISPANO HA-220

Dimensions: Span, 34 ft 2 in (10,42 m), over tip-tanks, 35 ft 10 in (10,93 m); length, 29 ft 5 in (8,97 m); height, 9 ft 4 in (2,85 m); wing area, 187·2 sq ft (17,4 m²).

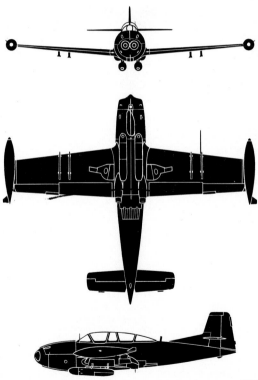

IAI-101 ARAVA

Country of Origin: Israel.

Type: Light STOL general-purpose transport.

Power Plant: Two 715 eshp Pratt & Whitney PT6A-27 turboprops.

Performance: Max. speed, 217 mph (350 km/h) at 10,000 ft (3 050 m); econ. cruise, 209 mph (337 km/h) at 10,000 ft (3 050 m); range with max. fuel and 1,774-lb (805-kg) payload plus 30 min reserves, 867 mls (1 395 km), with max. payload and same reserves, 301 mls (486 km); initial climb, 1,715 ft/min (8,7 m/sec); service ceiling, 28,550 ft (8 700 m).

Weights: Empty equipped (utility), 7,343 lb (3 330 kg), (commuter), 7,790 lb (3 533 kg); max. take-off, 12,500 lb (5 670 kg).

Accommodation: Flight crew of one or two, and (commuter version) up to 20 passengers in four-abreast rows. Aeromedical layout for 12 casualty stretchers and medical attendants.

Status: First of two prototypes flown on November 27, 1969. Six pre-production examples to be completed during 1971 with production deliveries scheduled to commence early 1972 when a production rate of four per month is anticipated.

Notes: Stretched version of the Arava accommodating up to 32 passengers currently envisaged.

126

IAI-101 ARAVA

Dimensions: Span, 69 ft 6 in (20,88 m); length, 42 ft 7½ in (12,99 m); height, 17 ft 0¾ in (5,20 m); wing area, 470·2 sq ft (43,68 m²).

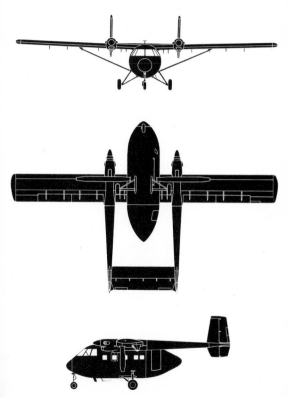

IAI COMMODORE JET 1123

Country of Origin: Israel.

Type: Light business executive transport.

Power Plant: Two 3,100 lb (1 406 kg) General Electric CJ610-9 turbojets.

Performance: Max. speed, 541 mph (871 km/h) at 19,500 ft (5 944 m); econ. cruise, 420 mph (676 km/h) at 41,000 ft (12 500 m); range with max. fuel and 45 min reserves, 2,000 mls (3 218 km), with 2,000-lb (907-kg) payload and same reserves, 1,450 mls (2 333 km); max. initial climb, 4,100 ft/min (20,83 m/sec); service ceiling, 45,000 ft (13 715 m).

Weights: Basic operational, 11,070 lb (5 021 kg); max. take-off, 20,800 lb (9 434 kg).

Accommodation: Normal flight crew of two and maximum of 10 passengers.

Status: First prototype (modified Jet Commander 1121) flown January 1970, and definitive prototype flown September 28, 1970. First production Commodore Jet 1123 was scheduled to fly early 1971 with 24 scheduled for delivery during course of year and production tempo of three per month being attained in 1972.

Notes: Commodore Jet 1123 is derivative of Aero Commander Jet Commander 1121 (see 1966 edition) of which 149 built in USA. Tooling and jigs transferred to Israel where fuselage extended 22 in (55 cm), double-slotted Fowler-type flaps, wing leading-edge droop, lift dumpers, permanent wingtip tanks, more powerful turbojet, and other modifications have been introduced.

IAI COMMODORE JET 1123

Dimensions: Span, 44 ft 9½ in (13,65 m); length, 52 ft 3 in (15,92 m); height, 15 ft 9½ in (4,81 m); wing area, 303·3 sq ft (28,18 m²).

ILYUSHIN IL-62 (CLASSIC)

Country of Origin: USSR.

Type: Long-range commercial transport.

Power Plant: Four 23,150 lb (10 500 kg) Kuznetsov NK-8-4 turbofans.

Performance: Max. cruise, 560 mph (900 km/h) at 29,500 ft (8 990 m); range cruise, 515 mph (830 km/h) at 36,090 ft (11 000 m); range with max. fuel, one hour's reserves and 22,050-lb (10 000-kg) payload, 5,715 mls (9 200 km), with max. payload and same reserves, 4,160 mls (6 700 km); initial climb at 352,740 lb (160 000 kg), 3,543 ft/min (18 m/sec).

Weights: Empty, 146,390 lb (66 400 kg); empty operational, 153,000 lb (69 400 kg); max. take-off, 357,000 lb (162 000 kg).

Accommodation: Normal flight crew of five, and alternative arrangements for 168 passengers in all-tourist configuration, 115 first-class passengers, or 186 passengers in high-density configuration.

Status: First of two prototypes flown January 1963, these being followed by three pre-production aircraft, production deliveries to *Aeroflot* commencing 1967.

Notes: Development of a high-density model, the Il-62M with uprated NK-8-8 turbofans, was proceeding at the beginning of 1971. The Il-62M is intended to accommodate up to 204 passengers, and will possess a range of 5,157 mls (8 300 km) with maximum payload, maximum take-off weight being raised to 363,750 lb (165 000 kg).

ILYUSHIN IL-62 (CLASSIC)

Dimensions: Span, 142 ft 0¾ in (43,30 m); length, 174 ft 2½ in (53,12 m); height, 40 ft 6¼ in (12,35 m); wing area, 3,037·57 sq ft (282,2 m²).

IRMA IAR-822

Country of Origin: Rumania.

Type: Single-seat agricultural aircraft.

Power Plant: One 290 hp Lycoming IO-540-G1D5 six-cylinder horizontally-opposed engine.

Performance: (Agricultural configuration) Max. speed, 106 mph (170 km/h); cruise at 75% power, 98 mph (158 km/h); normal operating speed, 80 mph (129 km/h); endurance, 3 hrs; range with standard fuel and without agricultural equipment, 310 mls (500 km); initial climb at 4,188 lb (1 900 kg), 690 ft/min (3,5 m/sec).

Weights: Empty (sprayer), 2,425 lb (1 100 kg), (duster), 2,469 lb (1 120 kg); max. take-off, 4,188 lb (1 900 kg).

Status: Prototype IAR-822 first flown autumn 1969 and pre-production batch of five under construction mid-1970.

Notes: The IAR-822 has been evolved from the IAR-821 (see 1969 edition) from which it differs primarily in the type of power plant installed, the earlier aircraft having a 300 hp Ivchenko AI-14MRF radial. Twenty-five IAR-821 and -821Bs were built, the latter being a tandem two-seat training variant. A similar two-seat version of the IAR-822, the -822B, is currently projected. The IAR-822 has a container for up to 132 Imp gal (600 l) of chemical spray or 1,323 lb (600 kg) of dry chemicals, and is built by the Intreprinderea de Reparat Material Aeronautic (IRMA).

IRMA IAR-822

Dimensions: Span, 42 ft 0 in (12,80 m); length, 30 ft 10 in (9,40 m); height, 9 ft $2\frac{1}{4}$ in (2,80 m); wing area, 279·86 sq ft (26 m²).

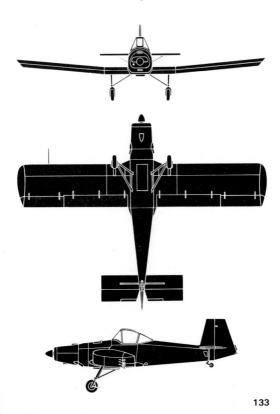

LET L 410 TURBOLET

Country of Origin: Czechoslovakia.
Type: Light utility transport and feederliner.
Power Plant: Two 715 eshp Pratt & Whitney PT6A-27 turboprops.
Performance: Max. cruise, 229 mph (370 km/h) at 9,840 ft (3 000 m); econ. cruise, 205 mph (330 km/h) at 9,840 ft (3 000 m); range with max. fuel and 45 min reserves, 705 mls (1 140 km), with max. payload and same reserves, 115 mls (185 km); initial climb rate, 1,595 ft/min (8,1 m/sec); service ceiling, 25,490 ft (7 770 m).
Weights: Empty equipped, 6,180 lb (2 803 kg); max. take-off, 11,245 lb (5 100 kg).
Accommodation: Basic flight crew of two. Configurations for 12, 15, 19 or 20 passengers in rows of three with two seats to starboard and one to port of aisle. Business executive layout available with accommodation for eight passengers.
Status: First of four prototypes flown April 16, 1969. Pre-production series of six aircraft to be built during 1971. First production deliveries (to CSA) to commence in 1972.
Notes: Principal production version of the Turbolet is to receive indigenous M-601-B turboprop of 740 eshp which was scheduled to commence flight testing early 1971. Latest modifications (see drawing) include redesigned wheel sponsons, a wider undercarriage track and revised engine nacelles.

LET L 410 TURBOLET

Dimensions: Span, 56 ft 1¼ in (17,10 m); length, 44 ft 7½ in (13,61 m); height, 18 ft 0½ in (5,50 m); wing area, 349·827 sq ft (32,5 m²).

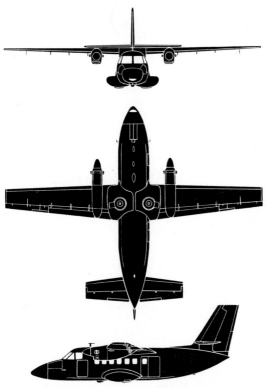

LOCKHEED 382G (L-100-30)

Country of Origin: USA.

Type: Medium- to long-range commercial cargo aircraft.

Power Plant: Four 4,508 eshp Allison 501-D22A turbo-props.

Performance: Max. cruise, 374 mph (602 km/h) at 25,000 ft (7 620 m); econ. cruise, 363 mph (584 km/h) at 28,000 ft (8 535 m); long-range cruise, 345 mph (555 km/h) at 28,000 ft (8 535 m); range with max. payload and 45 min reserves, 2,370 mls (3 814 km), with max. fuel, zero payload and same reserves, 4,830 mls (7 773 km).

Weights: Operational empty, 72,538 lb (32 903 kg); max. take-off, 155,000 lb (70 308 kg).

Accommodation: Normal flight crew of three and 6,057 cu ft (171,5 cu m) of cargo volume for loads of up to 45,000 lb (20 412 kg).

Status: First L-100-30 flown September 1970 with first deliveries (for Saturn Airways) scheduled for early 1971.

Notes: The L-100 is the commercial version of the military C-130 Hercules, variants including the Model 382B equivalent to the C-130E (see 1965 edition), the Model 328E (L-100-20) with a 100-in (2,54-m) fuselage stretch and 501-D22A engines, the Model 328F (L-100-20) with the lower-rated 501-D22s, and the Model 382G (L-100-30) with a further 80-in (2,03-m) stretch.

LOCKHEED 382G (L-100-30)

Dimensions: Span, 132 ft 7 in (40,41 m); length, 112 ft 8½ in (34,35 m); height, 38 ft 3 in (11,66 m); wing area, 1,745 sq ft (162,12 m²).

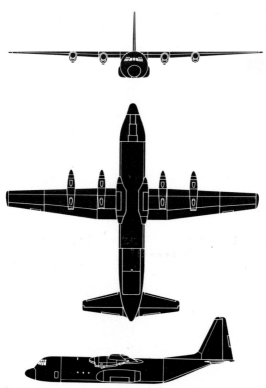

LOCKHEED C-5A GALAXY

Country of Origin: USA.

Type: Long-range military strategic transport.

Power Plant: Four 41,000 lb (18 600 kg) General Electric TF39-GE-1 turbofans.

Performance: Max. speed, 571 mph (919 km/h) at 25,000 ft (7 620 m); max. cruise at 525,000 lb (238 150 kg), 541 mph (871 km/h) at 30,000 ft (9 150 m); econ. cruise at 675,000 lb (306 175 kg), 537 mph (864 km/h) at 30,000 ft (9 150 m); range with max. fuel, 80,000-lb (36 287-kg) payload and reserves of 5% and 30 min, 6,500 mls (10 460 km), with max. payload and same reserves, 2,950 mls (4 745 km); initial climb at max. take-off, 2,300 ft/min (11,7 m/sec); service ceiling at 615,000 lb (278 950 kg), 34,000 ft (10 360 m).

Weights: Basic operational, 325,244 lb (147 528 kg); max. take-off, 764,500 lb (346 770 kg).

Accommodation: Basic flight crew of five plus relief crew and courier seating for 10. Seating for 75 troops on rear of upper deck, and provision for carrying 270 troops on lower deck. Typical freight loads include two M-60 tanks, an M-60 tank and two Iroquois helicopters, five M-113 personnel carriers, two Minutemen missiles on transporters, or 10 Pershing missiles with tow and launch vehicles.

Status: First of eight test and evaluation aircraft flown June 30, 1968, and first delivery to USAF made on December 17, 1969. Current orders for 81 C-5As scheduled for completion 1972.

Notes: USAF scheduled to have four C-5A squadrons.

LOCKHEED C-5A GALAXY

Dimensions: Span, 222 ft 8½ in (67,88 m); length, 247 ft 10 in (75,54 m); height, 65 ft 1½ in (19,85 m); wing area, 6,200 sq ft (576 m²).

LOCKHEED P-3C ORION

Country of Origin: USA.

Type: Long-range maritime patrol aircraft.

Power Plant: Four 4,910 eshp Allison T56-A-14W turbo-props.

Performance: Max. speed at 105,000 lb (47 625 kg), 476 mph (765 km/h) at 15,000 ft (4 570 m); normal cruise, 397 mph (639 km/h) at 25,000 ft (7 620 m); patrol speed, 230 mph (370 km/h) at 1,500 ft (457 m); loiter endurance (all engines) at 1,500 ft (457 m), 12·9 hrs, (two engines), 17 hrs; max. mission radius, 2,530 mls (4 075 km), with 3 hrs on station at 1,500 ft (457 m), 1,933 mls (3 110 km); service ceiling, 28,300 ft (8 625 m).

Weights: Empty, 62,000 lb (28 123 kg); normal max. take-off, 133,500 lb (60 558 kg); max. overload, 142,000 lb (64 410 kg).

Accommodation: Normal flight crew of 10 of which five housed in tactical compartment. Up to 50 combat troops and up to 4,000 lb (1 814 kg) of equipment may be carried in the emergency trooping role.

Armament: Weapons bay can house two Mk. 101 nuclear depth bombs and four Mk. 43, 44 or 46 torpedoes, or eight Mk. 54 bombs. An external ordnance load of up to 13,713 lb (6 220 kg) may be carried by nine pylons.

Status: YP-3C prototype flown October 8, 1968, with P-3C production deliveries commencing to US Navy mid-1969.

Notes: P-3C differs from P-3B (see 1969 edition) primarily in having new avionic equipment.

LOCKHEED P-3C ORION

Dimensions: Span, 99 ft 8 in (30,37 m); length, 116 ft 10 in (35,61 m); height, 33 ft 8½ in (10,29 m); wing area, 1,300 sq ft (120,77 m²).

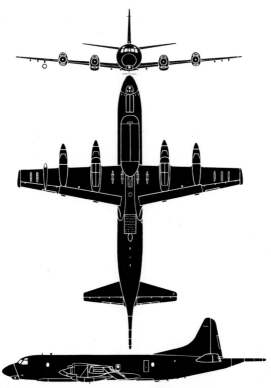

LOCKHEED F-104S STARFIGHTER

Country of Origin: USA.

Type: Single-seat interceptor and strike fighter.

Power Plant: One 11,870 lb (5 385 kg) dry and 17,900 lb (8 120 kg) reheat General Electric J79-GE-19 turbojet.

Performance: Max. speed, 910 mph (1 470 km/h) or Mach 1·2 at sea level, 1,450 mph (2 335 km/h) or Mach 2·2 at 36,000 ft (10 970 m); max. cruise, 610 mph (980 km/h) at 36,000 ft (10 970 m); tactical radius with two 162 Imp gal (736 l) and two 100 Imp gal (455 l) drop tanks, 740–775 mls (1 190–1 245 km); ferry range, 1,815 mls (2 920 km); initial climb, 50,000 plus ft/min (254 plus m/sec).

Weights: Empty, 14,573 lb (6 610 kg); loaded (clean), 21,307 lb (9 665 kg); max. take-off, 31,000 lb (14 060 kg).

Armament: One 20-mm M-61 rotary cannon, two AIM-7 Sparrow III and two AIM-9 Sidewinder AAMs.

Status: First of two Lockheed-built F-104S prototypes flown December 1966, and first Fiat-built production F-104S flown December 30, 1968. Production of 165 for Italian Air Force to be completed by end of 1972.

Notes: Derivative of the F-104G (see 1966 edition) optimised for all-weather intercept role. Features uprated engine with redesigned afterburner. Nine external stores attachment points. Primary armament is the Sparrow semi-active radar-homing AAM.

LOCKHEED F-104S STARFIGHTER

Dimensions: Span, 21 ft 11 in (6,68 m); length, 54 ft 9 in (16,69 m); height, 13 ft 6 in (4,11 m); wing area, 196·1 sq ft (18,22 m²).

LOCKHEED L-1011-1 TRISTAR

Country of Origin: USA.

Type: Short- to medium-range commercial transport.

Power Plant: Three 40,600 lb (18 415 kg) Rolls-Royce RB.211-22 turbofans.

Performance: (Estimated) Max. cruise at 360,000 lb (163 290 kg), 590 mph (950 km/h) at 35,000 ft (10 670 m); econ. cruise, 540 mph (870 km/h) at 35,000 ft (10 670 m); range with max. fuel and 40,000 lb (18 145 kg) payload, 3,915 mls (6 300 km); range with max. payload comprising 256 passengers and 5,000 lb (2 270 kg) cargo, 3,287 mls (5 290 km); initial climb, 2,800 ft/min (14,2 m/sec); service ceiling, 35,000 ft (10 670 m).

Weights: Empty, 208,782 lb (94 703 kg); operational empty, 223,904 lb (101 561 kg); max. take-off, 409,000 lb (185 552 kg).

Accommodation: Basic flight crew of three—four. Typical passenger configuration provides 256 seats in a ratio of 20% first class and 80% coach class. An all-economy configuration provides for 345 passengers, while up to 400 will be accommodated in a high-density configuration.

Status: First L-1011-1 flown November 16, 1970. Second was scheduled to join flight test programme mid-February 1971. First deliveries (to Eastern) scheduled for late 1971 by which time production rate is expected to be one aircraft per week.

Notes: The Model 193 (L-1011) TriStar is the first aircraft to employ the RB.211 engine, and uncertainty concerning an uprated -50 series of this engine was delaying a decision concerning extended-range TriStars at the beginning of 1971.

144

LOCKHEED L-1011-1 TRISTAR

Dimensions: Span, 155 ft 4 in (47,34 m); length, 177 ft 8½ in (54,16 m); height, 55 ft 4 in (16,87 m); wing area, 3,755 sq ft (348,85 m²).

McDONNELL DOUGLAS DC-8 SUPER 63

Country of Origin: USA.

Type: Long-range commercial transport.

Power Plant: Four 19,000 lb (8 618 kg) Pratt & Whitney JT3D-7 turbofans.

Performance: Max. cruise at 220,000 lb (99 800 kg), 583 mph (938 km/h) at 30,000 ft (9 150 m); long-range cruise, 512 mph (825 km/h) at 35,000 ft (10 700 m); range with max. payload and normal reserves, 4,500 mls (7 240 km), with max. fuel, 6,930 mls (11 150 km); initial climb, 2,165 ft/min (11 m/sec).

Weights: Basic operational, 153,749 lb (69 739 kg); max. take-off, 350,000 lb (158 760 kg).

Accommodation: Normal flight crew of four and up to 251 economy-class passengers plus 14,000 lb (6 350 kg) of freight.

Status: First DC-8 Super 63 flown April 10, 1967. Only Super 62 and 63 variants of the DC-8 remained in production at beginning of 1971 when approximately 540 DC-8s of all versions had been delivered.

Notes: The Super 63 is the ultimate development of the DC-8 family, being a combination of the fuselage stretch introduced by the Super 61, the aerodynamic improvements of the shorter-fuselage Super 62, and more powerful turbojets. All-cargo and cargo-passenger versions are known as the Super 63AF and 63CF Jet Trader, max. take-off weight being raised to 355,000 lb (161 028 kg). Similar variants exist of the Super 62 which has 18,000 lb (8 172 kg) JT3D-3B turbofans and a length of 157 ft 5 in (47,98 m).

McDONNELL DOUGLAS DC-8 SUPER 63

Dimensions: Span, 148 ft 5 in (45,23 m); length, 187 ft 4¾ in (57,12 m); height, 42 ft 5 in (12,92 m); wing area, 2,926·8 sq ft (271,9 m²).

McDONNELL DOUGLAS DC-9 SERIES 40

Country of Origin: USA.

Type: Short- to medium-range commercial transport.

Power Plant: Two 15,000 lb (6 804 kg) Pratt & Whitney JT8D-9 turbofans.

Performance: Max. cruise, 561 mph (903 km/h) at 27,000 ft (8 230 m); econ. cruise, 535 mph (860 km/h) at 33,000 ft (10 060 m); range cruise, 500 mph (805 km/h) at 35,000 ft (10 670 m); range at max. cruise with reserves for 230 mls (370 km) and 60 min hold, 1,192 mls (1 918 km), at range cruise with same reserves, 1,685 mls (2 710 km).

Weights: Empty, 59,690 lb (25 261 kg); max. take-off, 114,000 lb (51 710 kg).

Accommodation: Normal flight crew of two–three, and maximum of 125 tourist-class passengers in five-abreast seating.

Status: Series 40 first flown November 28, 1967, with first delivery (to SAS) following February 29, 1968. Deliveries of all models of the DC-9 totalled some 600 by the beginning of 1971 with 659 on order.

Notes: The DC-9-40 is a stretched version of the -30 (see 1968 edition) with more powerful turbofans and increased fuel capacity. A USAF aeromedical evacuation transport derivative of the DC-9-30 is known as the C-9A Nightingale (see 1969 edition), 21 examples having been ordered. Other models are the DC-9-10 (see 1966 edition), this being the initial basic version, and the DC-9-20 (see 1970 edition) for operation in hot-and-high conditions, combining the short (104 ft 4¾ in/31,82 m) fuselage of the -10 with the longer-span wing of the -30 and -40.

148

McDONNELL DOUGLAS DC-9 SERIES 40

Dimensions: Span, 93 ft 5 in (28,47 m); length, 125 ft 7¼ in (38,28 m); height, 28 ft 0 in (8,53 m); wing area, 1,000·7 sq ft (92,97 m²).

McDONNELL DOUGLAS DC-10 SERIES 10

Country of Origin: USA.

Type: Short- to medium-range commercial transport.

Power Plant: Three 40,000 lb (18 144 kg) General Electric CF6-6 turbofans.

Performance: Max. cruise, 585 mph (940 km/h) at 31,000 ft (9 450 m); range cruise, 520 mph (837 km/h) at 31,000 ft (9 450 m); range with max. payload, 2,760 mls (4 440 km) at 540 mph (870 km/h) at 35,000 ft (10 670 m), with max. fuel, 4,490 mls (7 225 km).

Weights: Operational empty, 230,323 lb (104 476 kg); max. take-off, 410,000 lb (185 970 kg).

Accommodation: Basic flight crew of three-four. Typical mixed-class arrangement will provide for 48 first-class and 222 coach-class passengers in six-abreast and eight-abreast seating respectively. A 332-passenger all-tourist arrangement is available.

Status: First DC-10 flown on August 29, 1970, and first deliveries (to American and United) scheduled for August 1971. Twelve DC-10s are expected to have been delivered by the end of 1971 with a production tempo of two per month being attained late 1972.

Notes: Developments of the initial Series 10 include the extended-range Series 20 and a more powerful equivalent, the Series 30 with 49,000-lb (22 225-kg) CF6-50A engines. First deliveries of the Series 30 (to the KSSU consortium) scheduled for 1972.

McDONNELL DOUGLAS DC-10 SERIES 10

Dimensions: Span, 155 ft 4 in (47,35 m); length, 181 ft 5 in (55,29 m); height, 58 ft 1 in (17,70 m); wing area, 3,550 sq ft (329,8 m²).

McDONNELL DOUGLAS (F-4M) PHANTOM F.G.R. MK. 2

Country of Origin: USA.

Type: Two-seat all-weather multi-purpose fighter.

Power Plant: Two 12,250 lb (5 556 kg) dry and 20,515 lb (9 305 kg) reheat Rolls-Royce RB.168-25R Spey Mk. 202 turbofans.

Performance: Max. speed, 910 mph (1 464 km/h) or Mach 1·2 at 1,000 ft (305 m), 1,386 mph (2 230 km/h) or Mach 2·1 at 40,000 ft (12 190 m); tactical radius with six 1,000-lb (453,6-kg) bombs and two 308 Imp gal (1 400 l) drop tanks for hi-lo-hi mission profile, 550 mls (885 km), lo-lo-hi mission profile, 380 mls (610 km); ferry range with max. external fuel, 2,500 mls (4 023 km).

Weights: Approx. empty equipped, 30,000 lb (13 610 kg); approx. normal loaded, 49,000 lb (22 225 kg); max. take-off, 58,000 lb (26 310 kg).

Armament: (Intercept) One 20-mm M-61A1 rotary cannon in SUU 23A centreline pod, four AIM-7E Sparrow IIIB and four AIM-9D Sidewinder IC AAMs, or (attack) 11 1,000-lb (453,6-kg) Mk. 14 bombs, 10 Matra pods each with 18 68-mm rockets, Martel ASMs, etc.

Status: First of two (YF-4M) prototypes flown February 17, 1967, and deliveries of 146 (F-4M) to RAF commenced July 1968 and completed October 1969.

Notes: Anglicised shore-based equivalent of US Navy's F-4J for RAF. Shipboard interceptor equivalent for the Royal Navy, the (F-4K) Phantom F.G. Mk. 1 (24 delivered), to be transferred to RAF. EMI reconnaissance pod being provided for RAF Phantoms during 1971.

McDONNELL DOUGLAS (F-4M) PHANTOM
F.G.R. MK. 2

Dimensions: Span, 38 ft 4¾ in (11,70 m); length, 57 ft 11 in (17,65 m); height, 16 ft 3⅓ in (4,96 m); wing area, 530 sq ft (49,2 m²).

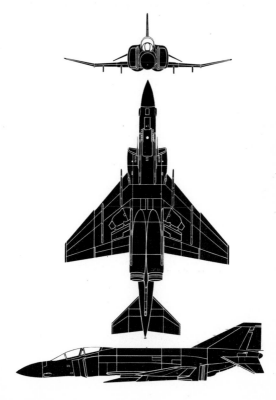

McDONNELL DOUGLAS RF-4E
PHANTOM II

Country of Origin: USA.

Type: Two-seat tactical reconnaissance aircraft.

Power Plant: Two 11,870 lb (5 385 kg) dry and 17,900 lb (8 120 kg) reheat General Electric J79-GE-17 turbojets.

Performance: Max. speed without external stores, 910 mph (1 464 km/h) or Mach 1·2 at 1,000 ft (305 m), 1,500 mph (2 414 km/h) or Mach 2·27 at 40,000 ft (12 190 m); tactical radius for hi-lo-hi mission profile with one 500 Imp gal (2 273 l) and two 308 Imp gal (1 400 l) drop tanks, 685 mls (1 100 km); max. ferry range, 2,300 mls (3 700 km) at 575 mph (925 km/h) at 40,000 ft (12 190 m).

Weights: Normal loaded, 46,076 lb (20 900 kg); max. take-off, 57,320 lb (26 000 kg).

Status: First production RF-4Es (six to Israel) delivered 1969, and first deliveries (of 88) to Federal Germany initiated November 1970.

Notes: The RF-4E is a multi-sensor reconnaissance version of the F-4E multi-purpose fighter (see 1970 edition) with the same engines, equipment standards being similar to those of the USAF's RF-4C (see 1965 edition) apart (in the case of Federal Germany's RF-4Es) from having a more advanced Goodyear side-looking radar and a data transfer system beaming reconnaissance data to ground stations. The *Luftwaffe's* RF-4Es will equip four 15-aircraft *Staffeln* which will operate from Bremgarten and Leck from late 1971. It is anticipated that 20 RF-4Es will be purchased during the early 'seventies to replace RF-86F Sabres serving with the Japanese Air Self-Defence Force. The US Marine Corps reconnaissance version of the Phantom is designated RF-4B.

McDONNELL DOUGLAS RF-4E PHANTOM II

Dimensions: Span, 38 ft 4¾ in (11,70 m); length, 62 ft 10½ in (19,20 m); height, 16 ft 3⅓ in (4,96 m); wing area, 530 sq ft (49,2 m²).

McDONNELL DOUGLAS A-4M SKYHAWK

Country of Origin: USA.

Type: Single-seat light attack bomber.

Power Plant: One 11,200 lb (5 080 kg) Pratt & Whitney J52-P-408A turbojet.

Performance: Max. speed without external stores, 685 mph (1 102 km/h) or Mach 0·9 at sea level, 640 mph (1 030 km/h) at 25,000 ft (7 620 m), in high drag configuration, 625 mph (1 080 km/h) or Mach 0·82 at sea level, 605 mph (973 km/h) or Mach 0·84 at 30,000 ft (9 145 m); combat radius on internal fuel for hi-lo-lo-hi mission profile with 4,000 lb (1 814 kg) of external stores, 340 mls (547 km); initial climb, 15,850 ft/min (80,5 m/sec), at 23,000 lb (10 433 kg), 8,440 ft/min (42,7 m/sec).

Weights: Empty, 10,600 lb (4 808 kg); max. take-off, 24,500 lb (11 113 kg).

Armament: Two 20-mm Mk. 12 cannon with 200 rpg. Maximum of 9,195 lb (4 170 kg) stores distributed between five external stations.

Status: First of two A-4M prototypes flown April 10, 1970, and first production aircraft for US Marine Corps delivered November 3, 1970.

Notes: A-4M is basically similar to the A-4F (see 1970 edition), apart from new avionics and more powerful turbojet, offering improved short-field capability, combat manoeuvrability, climb and acceleration. Cannon ammunition capacity has been doubled, the cockpit canopy has been enlarged, and a braking chute has been introduced.

McDONNELL DOUGLAS A-4M SKYHAWK

Dimensions: Span, 27 ft 6 in (8,38 m); length, 40 ft 3¼ in (12,27 m); height, 15 ft 0 in (4,57 m); wing area, 260 sq ft (24,16 m²).

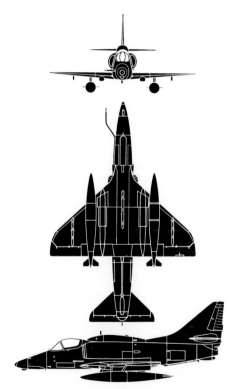

MBB HFB 330 HANSA FAN JET

Country of Origin: Federal Germany.

Type: Light business executive transport and feederliner.

Power Plant: Two 4,050 lb (1 840 kg) Garrett AiResearch ATF-3 turbofans.

Performance: (Estimated) Max. cruise, 550 mph (885 km/h) at 26,250 ft (8 000 m); range with 45 min reserves and four passengers, 2,800 mls (4 510 km), same reserves and 14 passengers, 2,025 mls (3 260 kg), with max. payload, 1,615 mls (1 600 km); time to 25,000 ft (7 620 m) at max. payload, 8 min; service ceiling at 18,500 lb (8 390 kg), 42,980 ft (13 100 m).

Weights: Operational empty, 13,670 lb (6 200 kg); max. take-off, 22,485 lb (10 200 kg).

Accommodation: Flight crew of two and business executive arrangements for 7–10 passengers. As a feederliner 14 passengers may be accommodated with an optional high-density arrangement for 16 passengers.

Status: The first prototype HFB 330 is scheduled to commence flight trials during 1971 with production deliveries commencing at a rate of one per month from November 1972.

Notes: The HFB 330 is essentially a stretched, re-engined development of the HFB 320 (see 1970 edition). The wing of the HFB 320 is retained unchanged, and there will be extensive commonality of other components.

MBB HFB 330 HANSA FAN JET

Dimensions: Span, 47 ft 6 in (14,49 m); length, 56 ft 9½ in (17,31 m); height, 16 ft 2 in (4,94 m); wing area, 324·4 sq ft (30,14 m²).

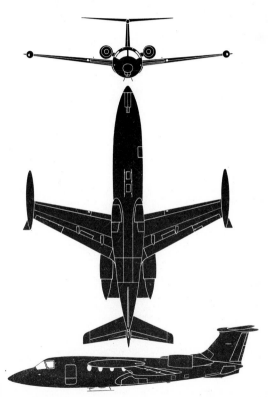

MFI-15B

Country of Origin: Sweden.
Type: Light air observation post and utility aircraft.
Power Plant: One 160 hp Lycoming IO-320-B20 four-cylinder horizontally-opposed engine.
Performance: Max. speed, 150 mph (241 km/h) at sea level; normal cruise, 129 mph (213 km/h); max. endurance at 118 mph (190 km/h), 4 hrs; initial climb, 1,083 ft/min (5,5 m/sec); time to 5,560 ft (2 000 m), 8 min; service ceiling, 14,765 ft (4 500 m).
Weights: Empty, 1,168 lb (530 kg); max. take-off, 1,929 lb (875 kg).
Accommodation: Side-by-side seating for two persons with space aft for 220 lb (100 kg) baggage or third (aft-facing) seat.
Status: Prototype flown as MFI-15A on July 11, 1969, and subsequently modified as MFI-15B in which form it first flew early in 1970.
Notes: A growth version of the MFI-9 intended as a fully-aerobatic trainer (MFI-15A) and as an air observation post and utility aircraft (MFI-15B), this aircraft is being tendered to fulfil a Swedish Army requirement. The MFI-15A (see 1970 edition) and MFI-15B are structurally similar, but the latter has a tailwheel undercarriage (in place of a nosewheel) and supplementary high-lift flaps to improve short-field performance.

160

MFI-15B

Dimensions: Span, 28 ft 6½ in (8,70 m); length, 22 ft 5¾ in (6,85 m); height, 6 ft 2¾ in (1,90 m); wing area, 134·5 sq ft (12,5 m²).

MIKOYAN MIG-21 (FISHBED-J)

Country of Origin: USSR.

Type: Single-seat multi-purpose fighter.

Power Plant: One 10,140 lb (4 600 kg) dry and 13,670 lb (6 200 kg) reheat Tumansky RD-11-300 turbojet.

Performance: Max. speed at 15,430 lb (7 000 kg), 1,450 mph (2 335 km/h) or Mach 2·2 at 39,370 ft (12 000 m), with 132 Imp gal (600 l) centreline drop tank and two Atoll AAMs, 1,055 mph (1 700 km/h) or Mach 1·6 at 39,370 ft (12 000 m); combat radius without external fuel at subsonic cruise, including acceleration to Mach 1·8 and five min combat above 39,370 ft (12 000 m), 390 mls (630 km); service ceiling, 55,775 ft (17 000 m).

Weights: Normal loaded, 18,300 lb (8 300 kg); max. take-off, 20,280 lb (9 200 kg).

Armament: (Intercept) Two Atoll AAMs plus 23-mm NR-23 cannon in centreline pod, or (ground attack) up to four UV-16-57 pods each containing 16 55-mm rockets, four 550-lb (250-kg) bombs, or four 220-mm or 325-mm rockets on underwing stations, plus centreline NR-23 cannon pod.

Status: Fishbed-J appeared in service with the Soviet Air Forces in 1968, being the latest known production derivative of the MiG-21PF all-weather interceptor (Fishbed-F, which see 1970 edition) which, in turn, was derived from the MiG-21F clear-weather interceptor (Fishbed-C, which see 1967 edition). Production of MiG-21 variants continues in Soviet Union, Czechoslovakia, and India.

Notes: Fishbed-J is a modified, more powerful development of earlier all-weather models (such as the Fishbed-D illustrated above), adding ground attack capability to the intercept role. It differs from the Fishbed-D and -F externally in having re-contoured aft decking, repositioned pitot head, and two additional underwing pylons.

MIKOYAN MIG-21 (FISHBED-J)

Dimensions: (Fishbed-C) span, 23 ft 5½ in (7,15 m); length with probe, 51 ft 8½ in (15,76 m), without probe, 44 ft 2 in (13,46 m); wing area, 247·57 sq ft (23 m²).

MIKOYAN MIG-23 (FOXBAT)

Country of Origin: USSR.
Type: Single-seat interceptor, strike and reconnaissance fighter.
Power Plant: Two (approx.) 24,250 lb (11 000 kg) reheat Tumansky RD-31 turbojets.
Performance: (Estimated) Max. short-period dash speed, 2,100 mph (3 380 km/h) or Mach 3·2 at 39,370 ft (12 000 m); max. sustained speed, 1,780 mph (2 865 km/h) or Mach 2·7 at 39,370 ft (12 000 m), 975 mph (1 570 km/h) or Mach 1·3 at 4,920 ft (1 500 m).
Weights: (Estimated) Normal loaded, 50,000–55,000 lb (22 680–24 950 kg); max. take-off, 70,000 lb (31 750 kg).
Armament: Probably internal weapons bay. Four wing weapons stations.
Status: Believed flown in prototype form 1963–64 with service deliveries following from 1967–68.
Notes: The MiG-23 multi-purpose fighter has established a number of FAI-recognised records since 1965 under the designation Ye-266, the first of these being announced in April of that year when a 621-mile (1 000-km) closed-circuit speed record of 1,441·5 mph (2 320 km/h), or Mach 2·2, with a 4,409-lb (2 000-kg) payload was established between 69,000 and 72,200 ft (21 000 and 22 000 m). On October 5, 1967, the Ye-266 established a record of 1,852·61 mph (2 981,5 km/h), or Mach 2·8, over a 310-mile (500-km) closed circuit, following this on October 27 with a speed of 1,841·81 mph (2 920,67 km/h), or Mach 2·7, over a 621-mile (1 000-km) circuit.

MIKOYAN MIG-23 (FOXBAT)

Dimensions: (Estimated) Span, 41 ft 0 in (12,5 m); length, 70 ft 0 in (21,33 m).

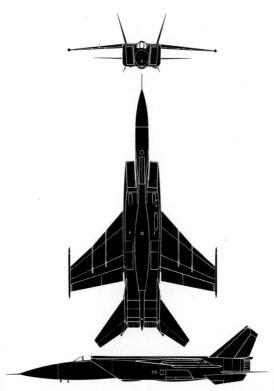

MITSUBISHI MU-2G

Country of Origin: Japan.

Type: Light business executive and utility transport.

Power Plant: Two 705 eshp Garrett AiResearch TPE 331-1-151A turboprops.

Performance: Max. cruise, 322 mph (518 km/h) at 10,000 ft (3 050 m); econ. cruise, 300 mph (482 km/h) at 20,000 ft (6 100 m); max. range with 30 min reserves, 1,550 mls (2 500 km) at 22,965 ft (7 000 m); initial climb, 2,592 ft/min (13,16 m/sec); service ceiling, 27,000 ft (8 230 m).

Weights: Empty equipped, 6,563 lb (2 977 kg); max. take-off, 10,802 lb (4 900 kg).

Accommodation: Normal flight crew of two, and various cabin arrangements providing accommodation for from four to 12 passengers.

Status: Prototype MU-2G flown January 10, 1969, deliveries of this model commencing during following autumn. Current civil production models are MU-2F and MU-2G, and total deliveries of all versions by the beginning of 1971 were approximately 190.

Notes: MU-2G is stretched derivative of MU-2F (see 1969 edition) with a 6 ft 2¾ in (1,90 m) increase in overall length, re-positioned nosewheel and external main undercarriage fairings. The MU-2J, which was under development late in 1970, marries the MU-2G airframe to uprated TPE 331 turboprops. Short-fuselage models include the initial MU-2B (see 1968 edition), the MU-2D with integral fuel tanks, and the MU-2C and -2D for the Self-Defence Forces, and four MU-2Gs have been ordered for the Air Self-Defence Force.

MITSUBISHI MU-2G

Dimensions: Span, 39 ft 2 in (11,95 m); length, 39 ft 5¾ in (12,03 m); height, 13 ft 8¼ in (4,17 m); wing area, 178 sq ft (16,55 m²).

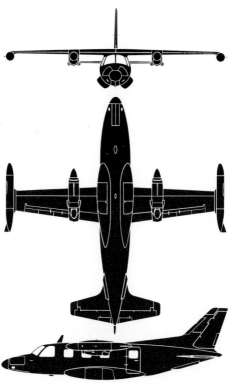

MITSUBISHI XT-2

Country of Origin: Japan.
Type: Tandem two-seat advanced trainer.
Power Plant: Two 4,600 lb (2 086 kg) dry and 6,950 lb (3 150 kg) reheat Rolls-Royce Turboméca RB.172-T.260 Adour turbofans.
Performance: (Estimated) Max. speed, 1,056 mph (1 700 km/h) or Mach 1·6 at 40,000 ft (12 190 m); max. ferry range, 1,600 mls (2 575 km); service ceiling, 50,000 ft.
Weights: (Estimated) Normal take-off, 21,000 lb (9 525 kg).
Armament: Provision for one 20-mm rotary cannon internally and various external ordnance loads on fuselage, underwing, and wingtip stations.
Status: First of two flying prototypes scheduled to be rolled out late July and to enter flight test phase September 1971. Current plans call for deliveries of 50 production T-2A trainers to commence 1973, with a follow-on order for a further 30 aircraft.
Notes: Japan's first indigenous supersonic aircraft, the T-2A trainer is intended to enter the inventory of the Air Self-Defence Force in 1974. The basic design is also intended to fulfil operational roles, and the ASDF has a requirement for 50 examples of a close-support fighter version, currently referred to as the SF-X, and for 20 examples of a short-range tactical reconnaissance model, the RF-X2, these entering the inventory from 1975 onwards. The first ASDF training squadron to receive the T-2A is scheduled to be formed during 1974, F-86F Sabres and T-33As currently used for advanced training being progressively withdrawn.

MITSUBISHI XT-2

Dimensions: Span, 26 ft 3 in (8,00 m); length, 55 ft 9 in (17,00 m); height, 16 ft 5 in (5,00 m); wing area, 215 sq ft (20 m²).

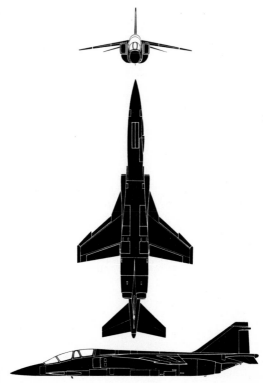

NAMC XC-1A

Country of Origin: Japan.

Type: Medium-range military transport.

Power Plant: Two 14,500 lb (6 575 kg) Pratt & Whitney JT8D-9 turbofans.

Performance: (Estimated) Max. speed, 507 mph (815 km/h) at 23,200 ft (7 600 m); max. cruise, 438 mph (704 km/h) at 35,100 ft (10 700 m); range with max. fuel, 2,073 mls (3 335 km), with (normal) 17,637-lb (8 000-kg) payload, 806 mls (1 297 km); initial climb, 3,806 ft/min (19,3 m/sec); service ceiling, 39,370 ft (12 000 m).

Weights: Empty equipped, 50,706 lb (23 000 kg); max. take-off, 85,980 lb (39 000 kg).

Accommodation: Basic crew of five. Loads include 60 troops, 45 paratroops, or 36 casualty stretchers plus medical attendants. Cargo loads may include a 5,000-lb (2 268-kg) truck, a 105-mm howitzer, two 1,500-lb (680-kg) trucks, or three jeep-type vehicles.

Status: First of two flying prototypes commenced flight test programme on November 12, 1970. Production deliveries scheduled to commence during the 1973 fiscal year in which four are expected to be built, production attaining one per month during 1974.

Notes: The C-1A is intended as a successor to the aged Curtiss C-46 in Air Self-Defence Force squadrons, the service having a requirement for 50 aircraft. A surveillance version is currently proposed.

170

NAMC XC-1A

Dimensions: Span, 101 ft 8½ in (31,00 m); length, 95 ft 1¾ in (29,00 m); height, 32 ft 9¾ in (10,00 m); wing area, 1,291·7 sq ft (120 m²).

NAMC YS-11A

Country of Origin: Japan.

Type: Short- and medium-range transport.

Power Plant: Two 2,660 ehp dry and 3,060 ehp wet Rolls-Royce Dark Mk. 542-10K turboprops.

Performance: Max. cruise, 291 mph (469 km/h) at 15,000 ft (4 575 m); econ. cruise, 281 mph (452 km/h) at 20,000 ft (6 100 m); range with max. fuel, 2,000 mls (3 215 km), with max. payload and without reserves, 680 mls (1 090 km); initial climb, 1,220 ft/min (6,2 m/sec); service ceiling, 22,900 ft (6 980 m).

Weights: Operational empty (-200), 33,942 lb (15 396 kg), (-300) 34,855 lb (15 810 kg); max. take-off, 54,010 lb (24 500 kg).

Accommodation: Basic flight crew of two, and (-200) up to 60 passengers in pairs on each side of central aisle, or (-300) 46 passengers plus 540 cu ft (15,29 m³) cargo space forward.

Status: First of two prototypes flown August 30, 1962, with deliveries (YS-11A-100) commencing March 1965. Production of 47 -100 series aircraft completed October 1967 and superseded by -200 series. YS-11A-200 first flown November 27, 1967. Deliveries of all versions approaching 150 at beginning of 1971.

Notes: Specification is generally applicable to YS-11A-200, mixed-traffic -300, and all-cargo -400 series, the -300 being illustrated on opposite page. Variants include the -206 ASW trainer (see 1970 edition) and the -207 ocean observation model (illustrated above). The latter, employed by the Maritime Safety Board, carried search and rescue equipment.

NAMC YS-11A

Dimensions: Span, 104 ft 11¾ in (32,00 m); length, 86 ft 3½ in (26,30 m); height, 29 ft 5¾ in (9,00 m); wing area, 1,020·4 sq ft (94,8 m²).

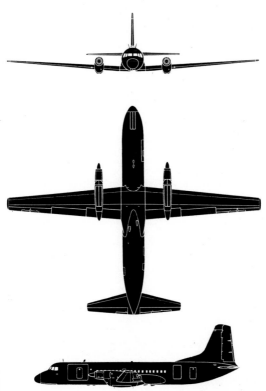

NORTH AMERICAN ROCKWELL
OV-10 BRONCO

Country of Origin: USA.

Type: Tandem two-seat (OV-10A) multi-purpose counter-insurgency and (OV-10B) target-towing aircraft.

Power Plant: Two 715 shp Garrett AiResearch T76-G-10/12 turboprops and (OV-10B) one 2,950 lb (1 339 kg) General Electric J85-GE-4 auxiliary turbojet.

Performance: (OV-10A) Max. speed without external stores, 279 mph (449 km/h) at sea level, 259 mph (417 km/h) at 20,000 ft (6 095 m); average cruise, 194 mph (312 km/h); tactical radius for close support mission at 12,500 lb (5 670 kg), 228 mls (367 km); ferry range, 1,380 mls (2 220 km).

Weights: (OV-10A) Empty, 6,893 lb (3 126 kg); take-off (clean), 9,908 lb; max. overload take-off, 14,444 lb (6 552 kg).

Armament: Four 7,62-mm M-60C machine guns with 500 rpg. Max. weapon load of 3,600 lb (1 633 kg) distributed between four 600-lb (272-kg) capacity and one 1,200-lb (544-kg) capacity external stations (on sponsons and beneath fuselage). Two 500-lb (227-kg) capacity wing stations optional.

Status: First of seven prototypes flown July 16, 1965. Production for US services comprising 157 for USAF and 114 for USMC completed April 1969. Manufacture resumed mid-1969 against order for 18 (OV-10B) for Federal Germany followed by 16 (OV-10C) for Thailand.

Notes: Twelve of 18 OV-10B target-tugs in process of delivery to Federal Germany are being fitted with an auxiliary turbojet (see opposite page) boosting max. speed to 375 mph (604 km/h). Installation features an "eyebrow" cover which is depicted closed.

174

NORTH AMERICAN ROCKWELL OV-10 BRONCO

Dimensions: Span, 40 ft 0 in (12,19 m); length, 39 ft 10 in (12,14 m); height, 15 ft 1 in (4,59 m); wing area, 291 sq ft (27,03 m²).

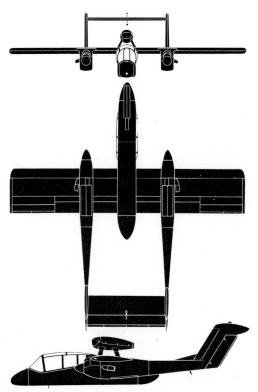

NORTH AMERICAN ROCKWELL RA-5C VIGILANTE

Country of Origin: USA.

Type: Tandem two-seat shipboard reconnaissance and attack aircraft.

Power Plant: Two 11,870 lb (5 395 kg) dry and 17,860 lb (8 120 kg) reheat General Electric J79-GE-10 turbojets.

Performance: Max. speed, 1,385 mph (2 230 km/h) or Mach 2·1 at 40,000 ft (12 190 m); max. stabilised speed without external stores, 1,254 mph (2 020 km/h) or Mach 1·9; max. low-level cruise, 633 mph (1 020 km/h) or Mach 0·83; long-range cruise, 560 mph (900 km/h) or Mach 0·85 at 40,000 ft (12 190 m); max. range with four 333 Imp gal (1 515 l) drop tanks, 2,995 mls (4 820 km); operational ceiling, 64,000 ft (19 510 m).

Weights: Normal max. take-off, 61,730 lb (28 000 kg); approx. max. overload take-off, 80,000 lb (36 285 kg).

Armament: RA-5C normally fulfils the reconnaissance role but possesses secondary attack capability with ordnance on four wing stations.

Status: First RA-5C flown June 30, 1962, and production phased out in 1963 but reinstated 1967 with order for additional 46 aircraft of which first flew March 1969 with completion of order scheduled for early 1971.

Notes: Derived from A-5A strategic bomber (see 1962 edition) via A-5B (see 1963 edition), both models being brought up to RA-5C standards, embodying extremely sophisticated reconnaissance system.

NORTH AMERICAN ROCKWELL RA-5C VIGILANTE

Dimensions: Span, 53 ft 0 in (16,15 m); length, 75 ft 10 in (23,11 m); height, 19 ft 4¾ in (5,90 m); wing area, 769 sq ft (71,44 m²).

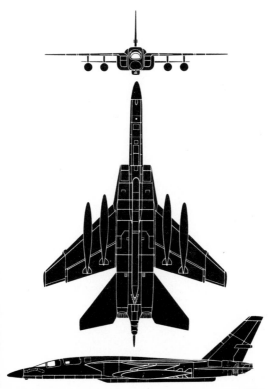

NORTHROP F-5-21

Country of Origin: USA.

Type: Single-seat air-superiority fighter.

Power Plant: Two 3,500 lb (1 588 kg) dry and 5,000 lb (2 268 kg) reheat General Electric J85-GE-21 turbojets.

Performance: (Estimated) Max. speed at 15,500 lb (7 031 kg), 720 mph (1 160 km/h) or Mach 0·95 at sea level, at 13,200 lb (5 988 kg), 840 mph (1 352 km/h) or Mach 1·1 at sea level, at 14,500 lb (6 577 kg), 1,055 mph (1 710 km/h) or Mach 1·6 at 40,000 ft (12 190 m); tactical radius for air patrol mission with three 229 Imp gal (1 040 l) external tanks, two Sidewinder AAMs, seven min loiter time and five min combat at 15,000 ft (4 570 m) using reheat, 805 mls (1 295 km); ferry range, 2,000 mls (3 220 km); initial climb at 16,050 lb (7 280 kg); 35,200 ft/min (179 m/sec).

Weights: (Estimated) Loaded (clean), 15,500 lb (7 031 kg); max. take-off, 24,140 lb (10 950 kg).

Armament: Two 20-mm M-39 cannon with 280 rpg and (intercept mission) two wingtip-mounted AIM-9 Sidewinder AAMs. Max. external ordnance load of 6,200 lb (2 812 kg).

Status: YF-5B-21 (illustrated above) flown March 28, 1969. F-5-21 selected as winning contender in USAF's International Fighter Aircraft (IFA) contest in November 1970. Production scheduled for 1971.

Notes: F-5-21 is more powerful derivative of F-5A (see 1970 edition) with air intercept radar, increased fuel capacity and aerodynamic refinements for Military Assistance Programme deliveries.

NORTHROP F-5-21

Dimensions: Span, 26 ft 6 in (8,08 m); length, 48 ft 5 in (14,76 m); height, 13 ft 2 in (4,01 m); wing area, 186 sq ft (16,28 m²).

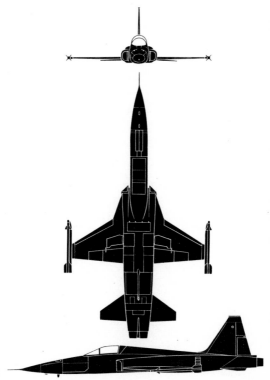

PARTENAVIA P.66B OSCAR-150

Country of Origin: Italy.
Type: Light semi-aerobatic training and touring monoplane.
Power Plant: One 150 hp Lycoming O-320-E2A four-cylinder horizontally-opposed engine.
Performance: Max. speed, 149 mph (240 km/h) at sea level; cruise at 75% power, 133 mph (215 km/h) at 7,000 ft (2 134 m); endurance at 75% power, 3 hrs; initial climb, 885 ft/min (4,49 m/sec); service ceiling, 14,760 ft (4 500 m).
Weights: Empty, 1,345 lb (610 kg); max. take-off, 2,050 lb (930 kg).
Accommodation: Two side-by-side seats with dual controls and third seat at rear of cabin.
Status: Latest addition to the Oscar family of light cabin monoplanes, the first prototype of which was flown on April 2, 1965 as the P.64 (see 1966 edition), the P.66B Oscar-150 and its two-seat counterpart, the Oscar-100, entered production in 1969. Some five–six Oscars of all versions were being manufactured monthly at the beginning of 1971.
Notes: The Oscar-100 and -150 are respectively two- and three-seat derivatives of the four-seat P.64B Oscar-180 and -200, most airframe components of the four models being interchangeable, primary differences apart from accommodation being the power plant installed, the Oscar-100 having a 115 hp Lycoming O-235-C1B, the -180 and -200 having a 180 hp Lycoming O-360-A1A and a 200 hp IO-360-A1A respectively. The P.64B is assembled in South Africa as the AFIC RSA 200 Falcon.

PARTENAVIA P.66B OSCAR-150

Dimensions: Span, 32 ft $9\frac{1}{4}$ in (9,99 m); length, 23 ft $3\frac{1}{8}$ in (7,09 m); height, 9 ft 1 in (2,77 m); wing area, 144·2 sq ft (13,4 m²).

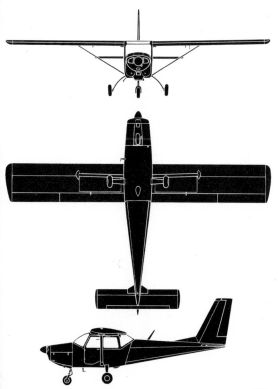

PARTENAVIA P.68

Country of Origin: Italy.
Type: Light utility transport.
Power Plant: Two 200 hp Lycoming IO-360-A1B four-cylinder horizontally-opposed engines.
Performance: Max. speed, 201 mph (324 km/h) at sea level; cruise at 75% power, 196 mph (316 km/h) at 8,200 ft (2 500 m), at 65% power, 194 mph (313 km/h) at 11,810 ft (3 600 m); range at 65% power with 30 min reserves at 55% power, 932 mls (1 500 km); initial climb, 1,850 ft/min (9,4 m/sec); service ceiling, 26,575 ft (8 100 m).
Weights: Empty, 2,216 lb (1 005 kg); max. take-off, 3,878 lb (1 760 kg).
Accommodation: Seating for pilot and five passengers in three pairs of side-by-side seats. Dual controls provided as standard equipment.
Status: First prototype flown on May 25, 1970, and series production is expected to commence during the course of 1971, the P.68 being offered with either 180 or 200 hp engines and either fixed or retractable undercarriage.
Notes: Placing emphasis on simplicity and ease of maintenance and operation, the P.68 possesses short-field capability and has been designed to fulfil such roles as air taxi, light utility transport, and ambulance. Modular design will permit manufacture of several variants without major changes in production facilities.

PARTENAVIA P.68

Dimensions: Span, 39 ft 4½ in (12,00 m); length, 29 ft 11 in (9,12 m); height, 10 ft 8 in (3,25 m); wing area, 200·2 sq ft (18,6 m²).

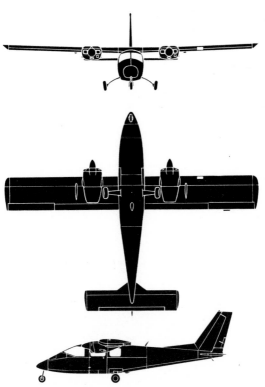

PILATUS PC-6D-H3 PORTER

Country of Origin: Switzerland.

Type: Light STOL utility transport.

Power Plant: One 500 hp Lycoming TIO-720-C1A eight-cylinder horizontally-opposed engine.

Performance: (Estimated) Max. cruise, 149 mph (240 km/h); econ. cruise at 60% power, 124 mph (200 km/h) at 1,000 ft (305 m); max. range with reserves, 838 mls (1 350 km).

Weights: Operational empty, 2,839 lb (1 288 kg); max. take-off, 5,512 lb (2 500 kg).

Accommodation: Basic arrangement for pilot with one passenger alongside and six passengers in individual seats in main cabin. High-density arrangement provides for up to nine passengers.

Status: First of five PC-6 prototypes flown May 4, 1959, and prototype of PC-6D-H3 flown April 2, 1970, with first customer deliveries being scheduled for early 1971.

Notes: The PC-6D-H3 is a new version of the long-established piston-engined Porter, embodying a more powerful engine and aerodynamic changes (e.g. vertical tail surfaces and wingtips) resulting from experience with the now-abandoned PC-8D Twin-Porter (see 1970 edition) programme. The Porter possesses an essentially similar airframe to that of the Turbo-Porter (see 1966 edition), and late in 1970 was being phased in to the three-per-month Turbo-Porter assembly line. Turbo-Porter versions include the PC-6A1-H2 (700 eshp Astazou XII), PC-6B1-H2 (522 eshp PT6A-20), and PC-6C1-H2 (605 eshp AiResearch TPE 331-25D).

PILATUS PC-6D-H3 PORTER

Dimensions: Span, 49 ft 8 in (15,13 m); length, 33 ft 5½ in (10,20 m); height, 10 ft 6 in (3,20 m); wing area, 310 sq ft (28,8 m²).

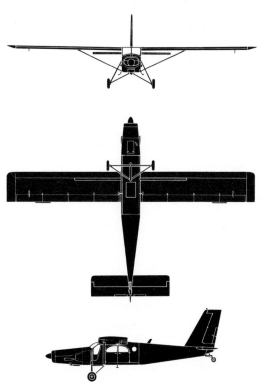

PIPER PA-31P NAVAJO

Country of Origin: USA.

Type: Light business executive transport.

Power Plant: Two 425 hp Lycoming TIGO-541-E1A six-cylinder horizontally-opposed engines.

Performance: Max. speed, 280 mph (451 km/h); max. cruise, 266 mph (428 km/h) at 24,000 ft (7 315 m); econ. cruise, 222 mph (357 km/h) at 24,000 ft (7 315 m); long-range cruise, 190 mph (306 km/h); range with max. fuel and no reserves, 1,410 mls (2 270 km) at econ. cruise, 1,480 mls (2 382 km) at long-range cruise; initial climb, 1,740 ft/min (8,8 m/sec); service ceiling, 29,000 ft (8 840 m).

Weights: Empty, 4,842 lb (2 196 kg); max. take-off, 7,800 lb (3 538 kg).

Accommodation: Standard arrangement for six individual seats in pairs with two additional seats optional. Alternative arrangement of seven individual seats with one additional seat optional.

Status: Prototype PA-31P flown in March 1968 with production deliveries commencing in March 1970.

Notes: The PA-31P is essentially similar to the PA-31-300 (see 1968 edition) and the Turbo Navajo apart from the introduction of cabin pressurisation equipment with fail-safe structure for the pressurised section of the fuselage. A version with Pratt & Whitney PT6A-27 turboprops, the PA-31T, is scheduled to fly in April 1971. The original PA-31 Navajo (300 hp Lycoming 10-540-M engines) was flown on September 30, 1964, deliveries commencing in April 1967, and the Turbo Navajo differs in having turbo-supercharged T10-540-A engines of 310 hp.

PIPER PA-31P NAVAJO

Dimensions: Span, 40 ft 8 in (12,40 m); length, 34 ft 6 in (10,52 m); height, 13 ft 0 in (3,96 m); wing area, 229 sq ft (21,3 m²).

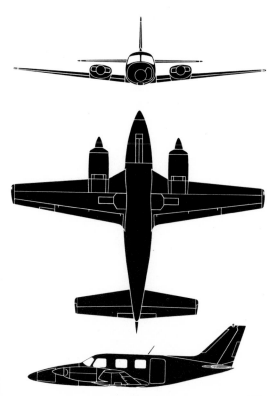

SAAB 35X DRAKEN

Country of Origin: Sweden.

Type: Single-seat multi-purpose fighter.

Power Plant: One 12,710 lb (5 765 kg) dry and 17,260 lb (7 830 kg) reheat Volvo Flygmotor RM 6C(Rolls-Royce RB 146 Mk. 60 Avon) turbojet.

Performance: Max. speed without external stores, 1,320 mph (2 125 km/h) or Mach 2·0 at 36,090 ft (11 000 m), with two 1,000-lb (453,5-kg) bombs and two 280 Imp gal (1 270 l) drop tanks, 925 mph (1 490 km/h) or Mach 1·4; tactical radius for hi-lo-hi mission profile without external fuel, 395 mls (635 km), with two 1,000-lb (453,5-kg) bombs and two 280 Imp gal (1 270 l) drop tanks, 620 mls (1 000 km); ferry range with four 280 Imp gal (1 270 l) drop tanks, 2,015 mls (3 245 km); initial climb, 34,450 ft/min (175 m/sec).

Weights: Loaded (clean aircraft), 25,130 lb (11 400 kg); max. take-off, 35,275 lb (16 000 kg).

Armament: Two 30-mm Aden M/55 cannon and up to 9,000 lb (4 082 kg) of ordnance distributed between nine external stations (six under wings and three under fuselage).

Status: Development airframe flown summer 1967, and first production Saab 35X (for Denmark) flown January 29, 1970.

Notes: The Saab 35X is an export version of the basic Draken (see Saab 35F, 1970 edition) ordered by Denmark and Finland. Denmark is in process of receiving 40 single-seat Saab 35XDs (illustrated) and six two-seat Saab 35XTs, and 12 single-seat Saab XSs have been ordered by Finland.

SAAB 35X DRAKEN

Dimensions: Span, 30 ft 10¾ in (9,40 m); length, 46 ft 10¼ in (14,28 m); height, 12 ft 8⅓ in (3,89 m); wing area, 529·6 sq ft (49,2 m²).

SAAB 37 VIGGEN

Country of Origin: Sweden.

Type: Single-seat multi-purpose fighter and two-seat operational trainer.

Power Plant: One 14,700 lb (6 667 kg) dry and 26,450 lb (12 000 kg) reheat Volvo Flygmotor RM 8 (Pratt & Whitney JT8D-22) turbofan.

Performance: (Estimated) Max. speed without external stores, 1,085 mph (1 745 km/h) or Mach 1·6 at 36,090 ft (11 000 m), 875 mph (1 410 km/h) or Mach 1·15 at 305 ft (100 m); tactical radius with typical external ordnance load for hi-lo-hi mission profile, 620 mls (1 000 km), for lo-lo-lo mission profile, 310 mls (500 km); time to 36,090 ft (11 000 m), 2 min.

Weights: Normal max. take-off, 35,275 lb (16 000 kg).

Armament: All ordnance carried on seven external stores stations (four beneath wings and three under fuselage), primary armament being RB 04C or RB 05A ASMs for the attack role, or RB 24 (Sidewinder), RB 27 or RB 28 (Falcon) AAMs for the intercept role.

Status: First of six single-seat prototypes flown February 8, 1967, and two-seat prototype (illustrated above) flown July 2, 1970. Orders placed by beginning of 1971 for 150 single-seat (AJ 37) and 25 two-seat (SK 37) Viggens. First production Viggen completed November 1970 and deliveries to Swedish Air Force scheduled to commence July 1971.

Notes: AJ 37 is primarily an attack aircraft with secondary intercept capability. Proposed versions include S 37 recce aircraft and JA 37 interceptor with variable intakes 2nd Mach 2·0 performance.

SAAB 37 VIGGEN

Dimensions: Span, 34 ft 9¼ in (10,60 m); length, 50 ft 8¼ in (15,45 m), including probe, 53 ft 5¾ in (16,30 m); height, 18 ft 4½ in (5,60 m).

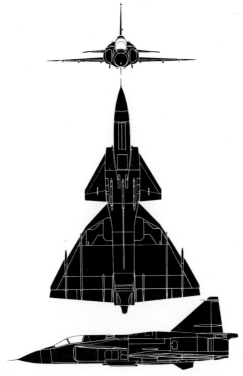

SAAB 105XT

Country of Origin: Sweden.
Type: Basic trainer and light strike and reconnaissance aircraft.
Power Plant: Two 2,850 lb (1 293 kg) General Electric J85-GE-17B turbojets.
Performance: Max. speed, 603 mph (970 km/h) at sea level, 543 mph (875 km/h) at 32,810 ft (10 000 m); range cruise, 435 mph (700 km/h) at 42,650 ft (13 000 m); range on internal fuel with 20 min reserves, 1,490 mls (2 400 km), with two 110 Imp gal (500 l) external tanks and 30 min reserves, 1,876 mls (3 020 km); tactical radius with six 500-lb (227-kg) bombs for hi-lo-hi mission profile, 514 mls (827 km), for lo-lo-lo mission profile, 200 mls (324 km).
Weights: Empty, 5,622 lb (2 550 kg); normal take-off, 9,822 lb (4 455 kg); max. take-off, 14,330 lb (6 500 kg).
Armament: Max. of 4,410 lb (2 000 kg) of ordnance distributed between six external wing stations.
Status: Prototype flown April 29, 1967, and first production deliveries (against order from Austria for 40) initiated July 1970.
Notes: The Saab 105XT is a more powerful, multi-purpose export version of the Saab 105 delivered to the Swedish Air Force (see 1968 edition) as the SK 60, this version having 1,640 lb (743 kg) Turboméca Aubisque turbofans. At the beginning of 1971 a further development of the export model, the Saab 105XH, was on offer to Switzerland, this having a semi-externally mounted 30-mm Aden cannon, 44 Imp gal (200 l) wingtip tanks, more advanced avionics, a modified wing, and a 15,432-lb (7 000-kg) max. weight.

SAAB 105XT

Dimensions: Span, 31 ft 2 in (9,50 m); length, 34 ft 5$\frac{1}{3}$ in (10,50 m); height, 8 ft 10$\frac{1}{4}$ in (2,70 m); wing area, 175·45 sq ft (16,3 m²).

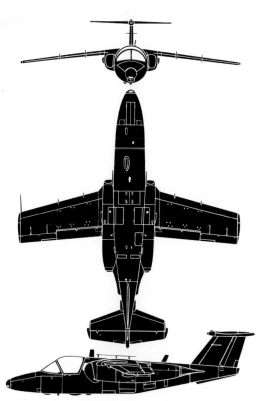

SCOTTISH AVIATION BULLDOG

Country of Origin: United Kingdom.
Type: Side-by-side two-seat primary trainer.
Power Plant: One 200 hp Lycoming IO-360-A1C four-cylinder horizontally-opposed engine.
Performance: Max. speed, 162 mph (261 km/h) at sea level; max. cruise, 153 mph (246 km/h) at 5,000 ft (1 525 m); econ. cruise, 148 mph (238 km/h) at 15,000 ft (4 570 m); max. range, 628 mls (1 010 km) at 4,000 ft (1 220 m); initial climb, 1,100 ft/min (5,58 m/sec); service ceiling, 20,000 ft (6 100 m).
Weights: Empty, 1,398 lb (634 kg); max. take-off, 2,350 lb (1 065 kg).
Status: Beagle-built first prototype flown May 19, 1969. Scottish Aviation-built definitive prototype was scheduled to fly early 1971 with first production aircraft following late autumn, production attaining six per month early 1972.
Notes: Originally designed by the now-liquidated Beagle Aircraft, the Bulldog has been taken over by Scottish Aviation, which is developing the aircraft for production. The initial prototype, essentially a modified Beagle Pup (see 1970 edition), illustrated on these pages differs in some respects from the definitive prototype, and production orders have been placed for the Kenya (five aircraft) and Swedish (58 aircraft with an option on 45 more) air forces. Scottish Aviation is investigating the possibility of introducing a high-lift slotted flap which, if successful, will be fitted to Swedish aircraft.

SCOTTISH AVIATION BULLDOG

Dimensions: Span, 33 ft 0 in (10,06 m); length, 23 ft 2½ in (7,07 m); height, 7 ft 5¾ in (2,28 m); wing area, 128·5 sq ft (11,94 m²).

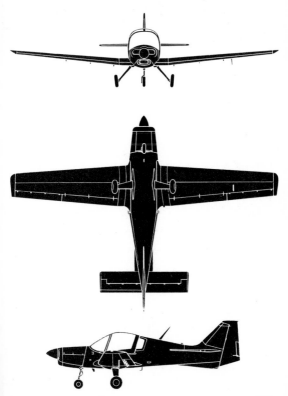

SEPECAT JAGUAR

Countries of Origin: France and United Kingdom.
Type: Single-seat tactical strike fighter and two-seat advanced trainer.
Power Plant: Two 4,620 lb (2 100 kg) dry and 6,950 lb (3 150 kg) reheat Rolls-Royce Turboméca RB.172-T-260 Adour turbofans.
Performance: (Estimated) Max. speed, 820 mph (1 320 km/h) or Mach 1·1 at 1,000 ft (305 m), 1,130 mph (1 820 km/h) or Mach 1·7 at 32,810 ft (10 000 m); cruise with max. ordnance load, 430 mph (690 km/h) or Mach 0·65 at 39,370 ft (12 000 m); tactical radius on internal fuel with typical load for hi-lo-hi mission profile, 775 mls (1 250 km), for lo-lo-lo mission profile, 405 mls (650 km); ferry range with max. external fuel, 2,800 mls (4 500 km).
Weights: (Estimated) Empty, 14,990 lb (6 800 kg); normal take-off, 22,046 lb (10 000 kg); max. take-off, 30,865 lb (14 000 kg).
Armament: Two 30-mm cannon and up to 10,000 lb (4 536 kg) ordnance distributed between five external stores stations (one under fuselage and four under wings).
Status: First of eight prototypes flown September 8, 1968. Five versions being developed simultaneously with production deliveries scheduled to commence in October 1971.
Notes: Both France and UK have requirement for 200 Jaguars, French variants being the single-seat A (*Appui Tactique*), M (*Marine*) and two-seat E (*École de Combat*), and British versions being the single-seat S (illustrated) and two-seat B, the RAF being intended to receive 164 single-seaters and 36 two-seaters.

SEPECAT JAGUAR

Dimensions: Span, 27 ft 10¼ in (8,49 m); length, 50 ft 11 in (15,52 m); height, 16 ft 10 in (4,88 m); wing area, 258·33 sq ft (24 m²).

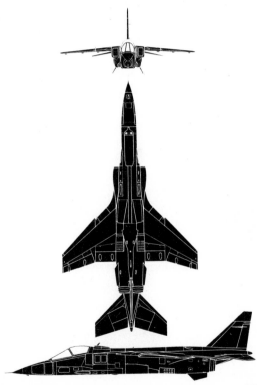

SHORT SKYVAN SERIES 3M

Country of Origin: United Kingdom.
Type: Light military utility transport.
Power Plant: Two 715 shp Garrett AiResearch TPE 331-201 turboprops.
Performance: Max. cruise, 201 mph (323 km/h) at 10,000 ft (3 050 m); econ. cruise, 173 mph (278 km/h) at 10,000 ft (3 050 m); range with max. fuel and 45 min reserves, 660 mls (1 062 km), with 5,000-lb (2 268-kg) payload and same reserves, 166 mls (267 km); initial climb, 1,520 ft/min (7,6 m/sec); service ceiling, 21,000 ft (6 400 m).
Weights: Basic operational, 7,400 lb (3 356 kg); max. take-off, 14,500 lb (6 577 kg).
Accommodation: Flight crew of one or two, and up to 22 fully-equipped troops, 16 paratroops and a despatcher, or 12 casualty stretchers and two medical attendants.
Status: Series 3M prototype flown early in 1970, and six delivered during course of year to Sultan of Oman's Air Force. Five ordered for Argentine Navy and one for Nepalese Army. Interspersed on assembly line with civil Series 3, and combined production running at one per month at beginning of 1971 with 53 ordered of both versions.
Notes: The Series 3M is the definitive military version of the Skyvan embodying features incorporated in two Skyvans supplied to the Austrian Air Force, optional nose-mounted weather radar (shown fitted on opposite page), and other new features.

SHORT SKYVAN SERIES 3M

Dimensions: Span, 64 ft 11 in (19,79 m); length, 40 ft 1 in (12,21 m), with radome, 41 ft 4 in (12,60 m); height, 15 ft 1 in (4,60 m); wing area, 373 sq ft (34,65 m²).

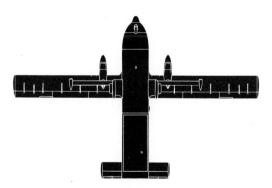

SIAI-MARCHETTI/FFA SA.202 BRAVO

Countries of Origin: Italy and Switzerland.

Type: Light training and touring monoplane.

Power Plant: One 150 hp Lycoming O-320-E2A four-cylinder horizontally-opposed engine.

Performance: (SA.202-15) Max. speed, 140 mph (225 km/h) at sea level; max. cruise, 130 mph (209 km/h); econ. cruise, 90 mph (145 km/h); range with max. fuel and no reserves, 685 mls (1 100 km); initial climb, 820 ft/min (4,16 m/sec); service ceiling, 13,000 ft (4 000 m).

Weights: Empty equipped, 1,336 lb (606 kg); max. take-off (aerobatic), 1,873 lb (850 kg), (utility), 2,204 lb (1 000 kg).

Accommodation: Two persons side-by-side with dual controls and optional aft seat for third person.

Status: Developed jointly by SIAI-Marchetti in Italy and FFA in Switzerland. First Swiss-built prototype flown March 7, 1969, and first Italian-built prototype flown May 7, 1969. Initial batch of 50 of SA.202-15 version under construction at beginning of 1971.

Notes: Several variants of the Bravo are projected, the initial production version, the SA.202-15, being described above. The SA.202-10 (represented by the first Italian-built prototype) has a 115 hp Lycoming O-235-C2A, and a prototype with a 160 hp engine was scheduled to commence its test programme late 1970. SIAI-Marchetti produces the fuselage, tail and controls, and FFA the wings, undercarriage and engine installation.

SIAI-MARCHETTI/FFA SA.202 BRAVO

Dimensions: Span, 31 ft 2 in (9,50 m); length, 21 ft 5½ in (6,54 m); height, 9 ft 1 in (2,77 m); wing area, 149 sq ft (13,86 m²).

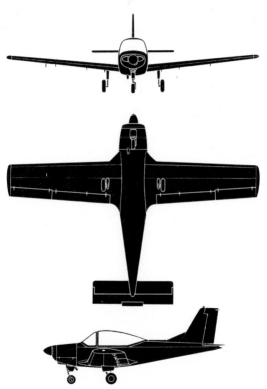

SIAI-MARCHETTI S.210

Country of Origin: Italy.

Type: Light cabin monoplane.

Power Plant: Two 200 hp Lycoming TIO-360-A1B four-cylinder horizontally-opposed engines.

Performance: Max. speed, 233 mph (375 km/h) at 18,700 ft (5 700 m); cruise at 75% power, 215 mph (346 km/h) at 18,700 ft (5 700 m); max. range, 1,180 mls (1 190 km); initial climb, 1,560 ft/min (7,92 m/sec).

Weights: Empty equipped, 2,359 lb (1 070 kg); max. take-off, 4,078 lb (1 850 kg).

Accommodation: Pilot and five passengers in three pairs of side-by-side seats.

Status: First of two prototypes flown February 18, 1970, and work initiated on pre-production series of 10 airframes.

Notes: A twin-engined derivative of the S.205–S.208 range of single-engined light cabin monoplanes and possessing extensive structural component commonality with its predecessors, the S.210 has been under development for several years, prototype trials being delayed by the priority attached to establishing the company's single-engined line. The second prototype differs from that illustrated above in having staggered entry doors (rear port, front starboard), an enlarged baggage compartment door, and enlarged rear windows.

SIAI-MARCHETTI S.210

Dimensions: Span, 38 ft 2 in (11,63 m); length, 28 ft 11$\frac{7}{8}$ in (8,83 m); height, 10 ft 1$\frac{3}{4}$ in (3,09 m); wing area, 185·5 sq ft (17,23 m²).

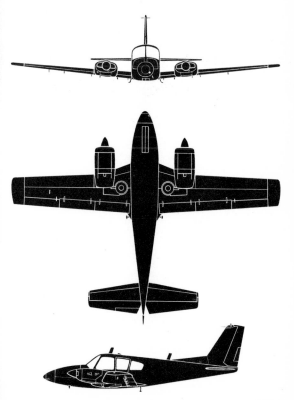

SIAI-MARCHETTI SF.260MX

Country of Origin: Italy.

Type: Primary training monoplane.

Power Plant: One 260 hp Lycoming O-540-E4A5 six-cylinder horizontally-opposed engine.

Performance: Max. speed, 230 mph (370 km/h) at sea level; max. cruise, 214 mph (345 km/h) at 10,000 ft (3 050 m); econ. cruise, 203 mph (327 km/h) at 10,000 ft (3 050 m); max. range (with two persons), 1,275 mls (2 050 km); initial climb, 1,770 ft/min (10 m/sec); service ceiling, 21,370 ft (6 500 m).

Weights: Empty (standard equipment), 1,543 lb (700 kg); max. loaded (aerobatic), 2,205 lb (1 000 kg); max. take-off, 2,650 lb (1 200 kg).

Accommodation: Two side-by-side seats with full dual controls, and aft bench-type seat normally occupied by one person.

Status: SF.260MX is the generic designation for the export military version of the SF.260 cabin monoplane originally developed by Aviamilano and flown in definitive prototype form in 1966. Deliveries of the SF.260MX commenced early in 1970.

Notes: Essentially similar apart from equipment to the civil SF.260, a second series of 50 of which were nearing completion at the beginning of 1971, this aircraft has been selected as an elementary trainer by the air arms of three countries, Belgium having ordered 36 (as SF.260MBs), the Congo having ordered 12 (as SF.260MCs) and taken an option on a further 12, and Zambia having ordered eight (as SF.260MZs).

SIAI-MARCHETTI SF.260MX

Dimensions: Span, 26 ft 11¾ in (8,25 m); length, 23 ft 0 in (7,02 m); height, 8 ft 6 in (2,60 m); wing area, 108·5 sq ft (10,1 m²).

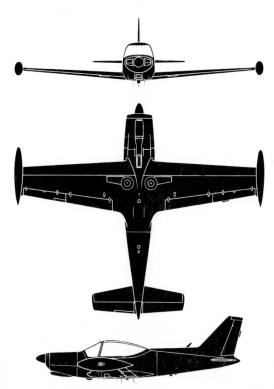

SIAI-MARCHETTI SM.1019

Country of Origin: Italy.
Type: Battlefield surveillance and forward air control aircraft.
Power Plant: One 317 shp Allison 250-B15G turboprop.
Performance: Max. speed, 188 mph (302 km/h) at 6,000 ft (1 830 m); max. cruise, 173 mph (278 km/h) at 6,000 ft (1 830 m); econ. cruise, 135 mph (217 km/h) at 10,000 ft (3 050 m); range with max. fuel and 10 min reserves, 765 mls (1 230 km), with 500-lb (227-kg) external stores on wing stations and same reserves, 320 mls (515 km); initial climb, 1,625 ft (8,25 m/sec).
Weights: Empty equipped, 1,480 lb (672 kg); max. take-off, 2,513 lb (1 140 kg).
Armament: Two stores stations under wings capable of carrying minigun pods, rockets, etc., up to a maximum external load of 500 lb (227 kg).
Status: First of two prototypes flown May 24, 1969 and second on July 14, 1970.
Notes: The SM.1019 is based upon the Cessna O-1 Bird Dog but possesses an extensively modified airframe to meet latest operational requirements, redesigned tail surfaces, and a turboprop in place of the O-1's piston engine. At the beginning of 1971 the SM.1019 was competing with the AM.3C (see pages 6–7) for a production order for the Italian Army.

SIAI-MARCHETTI SM.1019

Dimensions: Span, 36 ft 0 in (10,97 m); length, 27 ft 8 in (8,43 m); height, 7 ft 9¾ in (2,38 m); wing area, 173·94 sq ft (16,16 m²).

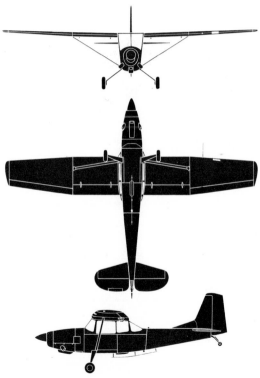

SOCATA ST-10 DIPLOMATE

Country of Origin: France.

Type: Light cabin monoplane.

Power Plant: One 200 hp Lycoming IO-360-C1B four-cylinder horizontally-opposed engine.

Performance: Max. speed, 186 mph (300 km/h) at sea level; cruise at 75% power, 168 mph (270 km/h); range with four passengers, 860 mls (1 385 km); initial climb, 1,005 ft/min (5,1 m/sec); service ceiling, 16,400 ft (5 000 m).

Weights: Empty equipped, 1,594 lb (723 kg); max. take-off, 2,690 lb (1 220 kg).

Accommodation: Pilot and three passengers in side-by-side pairs.

Status: First prototype flown November 7, 1967. Extensive modifications introduced prior to certification programme, type approval being received on November 26, 1969, with production deliveries commencing early in 1970.

Notes: Manufactured by the SOCATA (Société de Construction d'Avions de Tourisme et d'Affaires) subsidiary of Aérospatiale, the Diplomate employs a number of components common to the four-seat GY-80 Horizon which it supplants in the SOCATA range of light cabin monoplanes. Dual controls are standard and the Diplomate is claimed to be particularly suitable for airline pilot training.

SOCATA ST-10 DIPLOMATE

Dimensions: Span, 31 ft 9¾ in (9,70 m); length, 23 ft 9⅞ in (7,26 m); height, 9 ft 5½ in (2,88 m); wing area, 139·93 sq ft (13 m²).

SOCATA ST-60 RALLYE 7

Country of Origin: France.
Type: Light utility transport.
Power Plant: One 300 hp Lycoming IO-540-K six-cylinder horizontally-opposed engine.
Performance: Max. speed, 186 mph (300 km/h) at sea level; cruise at 75% power, 174 mph (280 km/h); range with max. fuel, 930 mls (1 500 km); initial climb, 985 ft/min (5 m/sec); service ceiling, 16,400 ft (5 000 m).
Weights: Empty equipped, 1,962 lb (890 kg); max. take-off, 3,946 lb (1 790 kg).
Accommodation: Side-by-side seats for two pilots or pilot and passenger, bench-type seat for three passengers and two staggered individual passenger seats at rear of cabin.
Status: Prototype flown for first time on January 3, 1969, the first pre-production example was flown on December 19, 1970, and development for series production was continuing at beginning of 1971.
Notes: Despite its name, the ST-60 Rallye 7 bears little relationship to the range of three- and four-seat Rallye light cabin monoplanes currently being manufactured by the SOCATA subsidiary of Aérospatiale. Combining such high-lift devices as leading-edge slats and slotted trailing-edge flaps with a relatively powerful engine, the ST-60 is claimed to possess exceptional short-field characteristics. The above specification relates to the proposed production model.

SOCATA ST-60 RALLYE 7

Dimensions: Span, 36 ft 1 in (11,00 m); length, 28 ft 8$\frac{1}{2}$ in (8,75 m); height, 9 ft 2$\frac{1}{4}$ in (2,80 m); wing area, 165·764 sq ft (15,4 m²).

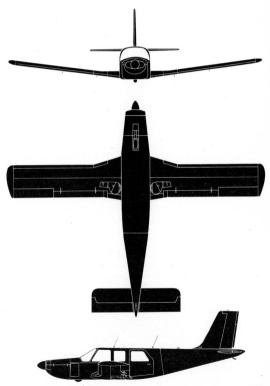

SOKO G-3 GALEB-3

Country of Origin: Yugoslavia.
Type: Tandem two-seat basic trainer and light strike aircraft.
Power Plant: One 3,395 lb (1 540 kg) Rolls-Royce Viper 20-F20 turbojet.
Performance: (Estimated) Max. speed, 515 mph (830 km/h) at 19,700 ft (6 000 m); max. cruise, 472 mph (760 km/h) at 16,400 ft (5 000 m); initial climb, 5,120 ft/min (26 m/sec); service ceiling, 39,370 ft (12 000 m).
Weights: Empty equipped, 6,327 lb (2 870 kg); max. take-off, 10,582 lb (4 800 kg).
Armament: Two 0·5-in (12,7-mm) Colt-Browning machine guns and underwing stores stations for 110-lb (50-kg) or 220-lb (100-kg) bombs, gun pods or ASMs.
Status: Prototype G-3 Galeb-3 flown May 1970 with production deliveries to Yugoslav Air Force scheduled for late 1971.
Notes: The Galeb-3 is a development of the basic G-2A Galeb currently equipping Yugoslav Air Force training schools. The Galeb (Gull) flew as a prototype in May 1961, series production of the G-2A version (see 1964 edition) with a 2,500 lb (1 134 kg) Viper 11 Mk. 22-6 commencing in 1963, some 150 being delivered to the Yugoslav Air Force, and four being supplied to Zambia, together with two examples of the single-seat Jastreb (Hawk) light strike derivative (see 1969 edition). The Galeb-3 embodies some structural strengthening, updated electronics and equipment, and increased external stores capability.

SOKO G-3 GALEB-3

Dimensions: Span, 34 ft 8 in (10,56 m); length, 33 ft 11 in (10,34 m); height, 11 ft 11½ in (3,64 m); wing area, 204·5 sq ft (19 m²).

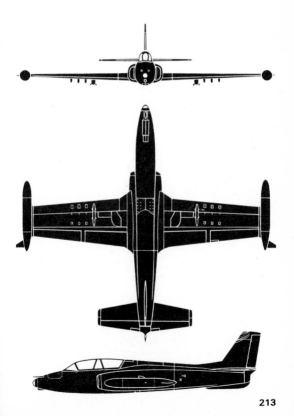

SUKHOI SU-7MF (FITTER)

Country of Origin: USSR.

Type: Single-seat ground attack fighter.

Power Plant: One (approx.) 22,050 lb (10 000 kg) reheat Lyulka AL-7 turbojet.

Performance: (Estimated) Max. speed without external stores, 720 mph (1 160 km/h) or Mach 0·95 at 1,000 ft (305 m), 1,056 mph (1 700 km/h) at 39,370 ft (12 000 m), in high-drag configuration (e.g. two rocket pods and two 132 Imp gal/600 l drop tanks), 790 mph (1 270 km/h) or Mach 1·2 at 39,370 ft (12 000 m); combat radius for hi-lo-hi mission profile, 285 mls (460 km); initial climb without external stores, 29,500 ft/min (150 m/sec).

Weights: (Estimated) Normal take-off, 26,455 lb (12 000 kg); max. take-off, 30,865 lb (14 000 kg).

Armament: Two 30-mm NR-30 cannon and such loads as two 550-lb (250-kg) bombs and two UV-16-57 pods each containing 16 55-mm rockets distributed between four external stores stations (two under wings and two under fuselage).

Status: Prototypes allegedly flown 1955 with production deliveries of initial service version to the Soviet Air Forces commencing 1958.

Notes: The Su-7 has been widely exported, the latest single-seat production model reportedly being the Su-7MF with up-rated engine and improved short-field characteristics. A tandem two-seat conversion trainer variant, the Su-7UTI, dubbed Moujik by NATO (see 1970 edition) is also in service.

214

SUKHOI SU-7MF (FITTER)

Dimensions: (Estimated) Span, 31 ft 2 in (9,50 m); length, 55 ft 9 in (17,00 m); height, 15 ft 5 in (4,70 m).

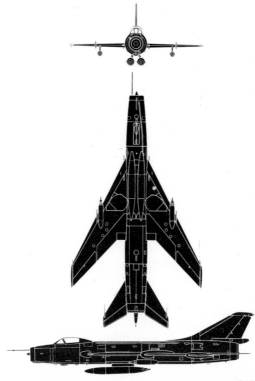

SUKHOI SU-11 (FLAGON-A)

Country of Origin: USSR.

Type: Single-seat all-weather interceptor fighter.

Power Plant: Two (approx.) 22,050 lb (10 000 kg) reheat Lyulka AL-7F* turbojets.

Performance: (Estimated) Max. speed without external stores, 1,650 mph (2 655 km/h) or Mach 2·5 at 39,370 ft (12 000 m), 910 mph (1 465 km/h) or Mach 1·2 at 1,000 ft (305 m), with AAMs on wing stations and twin drop tanks on fuselage stations, 1,120 mph (1 800 km/h) or Mach 1·7 at 39,370 ft (12 000 m); range at subsonic cruise with max. external fuel, 1,500 mls (2 415 km).

Weights: (Estimated) Normal take-off, 50,000–55,000 lb (22 680–24 950 kg).

Armament: Basic armament for intercept mission reportedly comprises two AAMs of Anab type on wing stations, but various ordnance loads may be carried for the attack role, these being distributed between two fuselage and two wing stations.

Status: The Su-11 is believed to have flown in prototype form during 1964–65 with production deliveries commencing 1967.

Notes: Apparently optimised for the intercept role as a successor to the Su-9 (see 1969 edition), the Su-11 is in large-scale service with the Soviet Air Forces. A STOL version with direct lift engines, the Flagon-B (see 1968 edition), is of uncertain status.

* It is possible that only pre-series or early production Su-11s were powered by the AL-7F, later aircraft having Tumansky RD-31s similar to those of the MiG-23.

SUKHOI SU-11 (FLAGON-A)

Dimensions: (Estimated) Span, 31 ft 3 in (9,50 m); length, 70 ft 6 in (21,50 m); height, 16 ft 6 in (5,00 m).

SWEARINGEN SA-226T MERLIN III

Country of Origin: USA.

Type: Light business executive transport.

Power Plant: Two 840 shp Garrett AiResearch TPE 331-303G turboprops.

Performance: Max. cruise, 316 mph (509 km/h) at 16,000 ft (4 875 m); econ. cruise, 296 mph (476 km/h) at 28,000 ft (8 535 m); range with max. fuel at econ. cruise with 45 min reserves, 2,710 mls (4 360 km); initial climb, 2,580 ft/min (13,1 m/sec); service ceiling, 28,000 ft (8 535 m).

Weights: Empty equipped, 7,200 lb (3 266 kg); max. take-of, 12,500 lb (5 670 kg).

Accommodation: Normal flight crew of two and standard accommodation for six passengers.

Status: Prototype SA-226T flown 1969 with production deliveries scheduled to commence late 1970 or early 1971. FAA certification awarded July 27, 1970.

Notes: Merlin III differs from the SA-26AT Merlin IIB (see 1970 edition) in having more powerful engines, redesigned tail assembly and an entirely new wing. The original production SA-26T Merlin IIA mated modified Beech Queen Air wings and Twin Bonanza undercarriage with a new pressurised fuselage and 550 shp PT6A-20 turboprops, the Merlin IIB having 665 shp TPE 331-1-151Gs and new pressurisation system.

218

SWEARINGEN SA-226T MERLIN III

Dimensions: Span, 46 ft 3 in (14,10 m); length, 42 ft 2 in (12,85 m); height, 16 ft 8 in (5,08 m); wing area, 277·5 sq ft (25,78 m²).

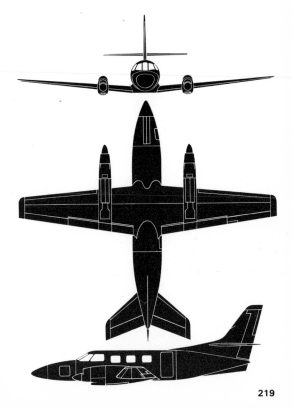

SWEARINGEN SA-226AT MERLIN IV

Country of Origin: USA.

Type: Business executive transport and (Metro) short-haul feederliner.

Power Plant: Two 840 shp Garrett AiResearch TPE 331-303G turboprops.

Performance: Max. cruise, 305 mph (491 km/h) at 16,000 ft (4 875 m); econ. cruise, 286 mph (460 km/h) at 28,000 ft (8 535 m); range with max. fuel at max. cruise, 1,890 mls (3 040 km), at econ. cruise with 45 min reserves, 2,550 mls (4 104 km).

Weights: Empty equipped, 7,700 lb (3 493 kg); max. takeoff, 12,500 lb (5 670 kg).

Accommodation: Normal flight crew of two and standard accommodation for 12 passengers, or (Metro configuration) basic accommodation for 20 passengers with convertible passenger/cargo interior.

Status: Prototype Merlin IV flown August 26, 1969. FAA certification granted September 22, 1970, with production deliveries scheduled for late 1970 or early 1971.

Notes: The Merlin IV is a stretched version of the Merlin III (see pages 218–219) with additional fuselage sections inserted fore and aft of the wing. It is being offered both as a corporate transport and as a commuter-type airliner for third-level operators, the latter version being known as the SA-226TC Metro and carrying 20 passengers over 200 mls (322 km).

SWEARINGEN SA-226AT MERLIN IV

Dimensions: Span, 46 ft 3 in (14,10 m); length, 59 ft 4¼ in (18,09 m); height, 16 ft 8 in (5,08 m); wing area, 277·5 sq ft (25,78 m²).

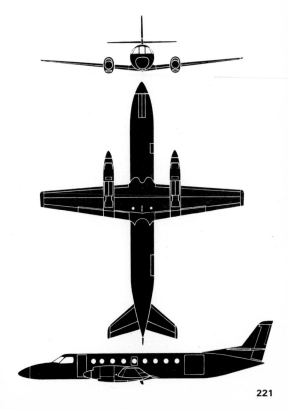

TRANSALL C. 160

Countries of Origin: France and Federal Germany.
Type: Medium-range tactical transport.
Power Plant: Two 5,665 shp Rolls-Royce Tyne R.Ty. 20 Mk. 22 turboprops.
Performance: Max. speed, 333 mph (536 km/h) at 14,765 ft (4 500 m); max. cruise, 319 mph (513 km/h) at 18,045 ft (5 500 m); range with 17,640-lb (8 000–kg) payload and reserves of 10% plus 30 min hold, 2,832 mls (4 558 km), with 35,270-lb (16 000-kg) payload and same reserves, 730 mls (1 175 km); initial climb, 1,440 ft/min (7,3 m/sec); service ceiling at 99,225 lb (45 000 kg), 27,900 ft (8 500 m).
Weights: Empty equipped, 63,400 lb (28 758 kg); normal take-off, 97,450 lb (44 200 kg); max. take-off, 108,250 lb (49 100 kg).
Accommodation: Flight crew of four and 93 troops, 81 paratroops, or 62 casualty stretchers and four medical attendants. Other possible loads include armoured vehicles not exceeding 35,270 lb (16 000 kg) total weight.
Status: First of three prototypes flown February 25, 1963, and first of six pre-production aircraft flown on May 21, 1965. Total orders for 169 production aircraft comprising 50 for France (C. 160F), 110 for Federal Germany (C. 160D), and nine for South Africa (C. 160Z), production being scheduled to phase out in 1972.
Notes: VFW-Fokker is overall Transall project manager, other participants being MBB and Aérospatiale.

TRANSALL C. 160

Dimensions: Span, 131 ft 2½ in (40,00 m); length, 106 ft 3½ in (32,40 m); height, 38 ft 4¾ in (11,65 m); wing area, 1,722·7 sq ft (160,1 m²).

TUPOLEV TU-22 (BLINDER)

Country of Origin: USSR.

Type: Long-range medium bomber and strike-reconnaissance aircraft.

Power Plant: Two (approx.) 27,000 lb (12 250 kg) reheat turbojets.

Performance: (Estimated) Max. speed without external stores, 990 mph (1 590 km/h) or Mach 1·5 at 39,370 ft (12 000 m), 720 mph (1 160 km/h) or Mach 0·95 at 1,000 ft (305 m); normal cruise, 595 mph (960 km/h) or Mach 0·9 at 39,370 ft (12 000 m); tactical radius on standard fuel for high-altitude mission, 700 mls (1 125 km); service ceiling, 60,000 ft (18 290 m).

Weights: (Estimated) Max. take-off, 185,000 lb (84 000 kg).

Armament: Free-falling weapons housed internally or (Blinder-B) semi-recessed Kitchen ASM. Remotely-controlled 23-mm cannon in tail barbette.

Status: Believed to have attained operational status with the Soviet Air Forces in 1965.

Notes: The Tu-22 is the successor to the subsonic Tu-16 in Soviet medium-bomber formations and with shore-based maritime strike elements of the Soviet Naval Air Arm. The basic version, dubbed Blinder-A by NATO, is illustrated above, the missile-carrying Blinder-B being illustrated on the opposite page. A training version, the Blinder-C (see 1970 edition), features a raised second cockpit for the instructor. Recent production models of the Tu-22 display a number of modifications, including an extended flight refuelling probe and enlarged engine air intakes, nacelles and exhaust orifices.

TUPOLEV TU-22 (BLINDER)

Dimensions: (Estimated) Span, 91 ft 0 in (27,74 m); length, 133 ft 0 in (40,50 m); height, 17 ft 0 in (5,18 m); wing area, 2,030 sq ft (188,59 m²).

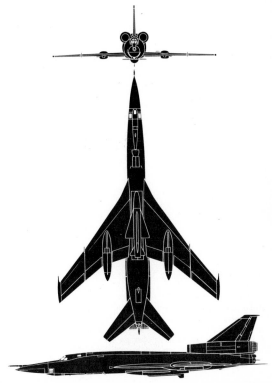

TUPOLEV TU-28P (FIDDLER)

Country of Origin: USSR.

Type: Two-seat long-range all-weather interceptor and reconnaissance-strike aircraft.

Power Plant: Two (approx.) 24,250 lb reheat turbojets.

Performance: (Estimated) Max. speed without external stores, 1,085 mph (1 745 km/h) or Mach 1·65 at 39,370 ft (12 000 m), with four Ash AAMs on wing stores stations, 925 mph (1 490 km/h) or Mach 1·4 at 39,370 ft (12 000 m); tactical radius for high-altitude patrol mission, 900–1,100 mls (1 450–1 770 km).

Weights: (Estimated) normal take-off, 78,000 lb (35 380 kg); max. take-off, 96,000 lb (43 545 kg).

Armament: Four infra-red or radar-homing Ash AAMs on wing stations for intercept role.

Status: The Tu-28 is believed to have flown in prototype form in 1957 and to have entered service in its Tu-28P interceptor version during the early 'sixties.

Notes: The Tu-28 is believed to have been evolved originally to fulfil a requirement for a long-range reconnaissance-strike aircraft, and its design was biased towards economical high-altitude operation. One version has been seen with a central pack that may be presumed to house early warning radar, and it is probable that an internal weapons bay is standard for the reconnaissance-strike role.

TUPOLEV TU-28P (FIDDLER)

Dimensions: (Estimated) Span, 65 ft 0 in (19,80 m); length, 90 ft 0 in (27,43 m).

TUPOLEV TU-134A (CRUSTY)

Country of Origin: USSR.

Type: Short- to medium-range commercial transport.

Power Plant: Two 14,990 lb (6 800 kg) Soloviev D-30-2 Turbofans.

Performance: Max. cruise, 528 mph (850 km/h) at 32,810 ft (10 000 m); long-range cruise, 466 mph (750 km/h) at 32,810 ft (10 000 m); max. range at long-range cruise with 1 hr reserves and 18,108-lb (8 215-kg) payload, 1,243 mls (2 000 km), with 8,818-lb (4 000-kg) payload, 2,175 mls (3 500 km).

Weights: Operational empty, 63,934 lb (29 000 kg); max. take-off, 103,617 lb (47 000 kg).

Accommodation: Basic flight crew of three and maximum of 80 passengers in four-abreast all-tourist class configuration.

Status: Prototype Tu-134A flown in 1968 and first production deliveries (to *Aeroflot*) mid-1970.

Notes: The Tu-134A differs from the original Tu-134, which entered *Aeroflot* service in 1966, in having an additional 6 ft 10⅔ in (2,10 m) section inserted in the fuselage immediately forward of the wing to permit two additional rows of passenger seats, and introduces engine thrust reversers. Maximum take-off weight has been increased by 5,512 lb (2 500 kg), maximum payload being raised by 1,025 lb (465 kg), an APU is provided, and radio and navigational equipment have been revised. Route proving trials with the Tu-134A were completed by *Aeroflot* late in 1970, and this airliner was to be introduced on international routes early in 1971. The shorter-fuselage Tu-134 serves with Interflug, LOT. Malev, Balkan-Bulgarian and Aviogenex.

TUPOLEV TU-134A (CRUSTY)

Dimensions: Span, 95 ft 2 in (29,00 m); length, 111 ft 0½ in (36,40 m); height, 29 ft 7 in (9,02 m); wing area, 1,370·3 sq ft (127,3 m²).

TUPOLEV TU-144 (CHARGER)

Country of Origin: USSR.

Type: Long-range supersonic commercial transport.

Power Plant: Four 28,660 lb (13 000 kg) dry and 38,580 lb (17 500 kg) Kuznetsov NK-144 turbofans.

Performance: (Estimated) Max. cruise, 1,550 mph (2 500 km/h) or Mach 2·35 between 49,200 and 65,600 ft (15 000 and 20 000 m); range with max. payload, 4,040 mls (6 500 km).

Weights: Max. take-off, 286,600 lb (130 000 kg).

Accommodation: Basic flight crew of three, and mixed-class arrangement for 82 tourist-class and 18 first-class passengers, or all-tourist arrangement for 121 passengers.

Status: First of two flying prototypes commenced flight test programme on December 31, 1968. Four pre-series aircraft were scheduled to join the development programme during 1970–71, and initial batch of 14 production aircraft reportedly under construction at beginning of 1971.

Notes: The Tu-144 possesses the distinction of having been the world's first commercial transport to exceed both Mach 1·0 (on June 5, 1969) and Mach 2·0 (on May 26, 1970), reaching 1,336 mph (2 150 km/h), or Mach 2·02, at 53,500 ft (16 300 m) during the latter flight. Like the competitive Anglo-French Concorde (see pages 34–35), the Tu-144 employs an ogival delta wing, a retractable vizor for cruising flight, and a droopable nose (see partly drooped above) for take-off and landing. It is intended that the Tu-144 be used on one-stop trans-Siberian services, and on some external services, including the Moscow–Delhi and Moscow–New York runs.

TUPOLEV TU-144 (CHARGER)

Dimensions: (Prototypes) Span, 81 ft 0½ in (24,70 m); length (excluding probe), 180 ft 5⅓ in (55,00 m).

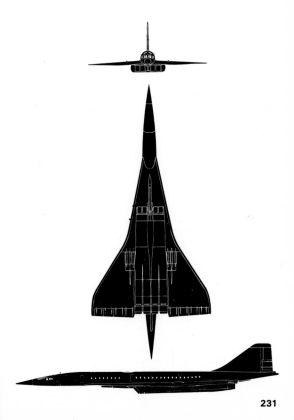

TUPOLEV TU-154 (CARELESS)

Country of Origin: USSR.

Type: Medium- to long-range commercial transport.

Power Plant: Three 20,950 lb (9 500 kg) Kuznetsov NK-8-2 turbofans.

Performance: Max. cruise, 605 mph (975 km/h) at 31,170 ft (9 500 m); long-range cruise, 528 mph (850 km/h) at 37,730 ft (11 500 m); range with standard fuel and reserves of 1 hr plus 6% and max. payload, 2,150 mls (3 460 km) at 560 mph (900 km/h), 2,360 mls (3 800 km) at 528 mph (850 km/h).

Weights: Operational empty, 95,900 lb (43 500 kg); normal take-off, 185,188 lb (84 000 kg); max. take-off, 198,416 lb (90 000 kg).

Accommodation: Basic flight crew of three–four, and alternative arrangements for 158 or 150 economy-class passengers, 150, 146 or 136 tourist-class passengers, or 24 first-class and 104 tourist-class passengers.

Status: First prototype flown October 4, 1968, with first delivery of a production aircraft (to *Aeroflot*) following August 1970.

Notes: The Tu-154, is scheduled to enter service on *Aeroflot* routes during the summer of 1971, is intended as a successor to the Tu-104, Il-18 and An-10 on medium- to long-range routes, and can operate from airfields with category B surfaces, including packed earth and gravel. A growth version, referred to as the Tu-154M, is currently under development with flight testing scheduled for 1971. This model will incorporate additional fuselage sections which will enable 220–240 passengers to be accommodated, and will have uprated NK-8 turbofans. Service introduction is planned for 1972–73.

TUPOLEV TU-154 (CARELESS)

Dimensions: Span, 123 ft 2½ in (37,55 m); length, 157 ft 1¾ in (47,90 m); height, 37 ft 4¾ in (11,40 m); wing area, 2,168·92 sq ft (201,45 m²).

VFW-FOKKER VAK 191B

Country of Origin: Federal Germany.

Type: Experimental single-seat V/STOL reconnaissance and strike fighter.

Power Plant: One 10,207 lb (4 630 kg) Rolls-Royce/MTU RB. 193-12 vectored-thrust turbojet and two 5,578 lb (2 530 kg) Rolls-Royce/MTU RB. 162-81 lift turbojets.

Performance: (Estimated) Max. speed, 730 mph (1 175 km/h) or Mach 0·96 at 1,000 ft (305 m), 605 mph (975 km/h) or Mach 0·92 at 39,370 ft (12 000 m).

Weights: Empty equipped, 11,695 lb (5 305 kg); max. (vertical) take-off, 17,626 lb (7 995 kg).

Status: First of three prototypes rolled out on April 24, 1970. First untethered flight trials were scheduled to commence early 1971, and all three prototypes are expected to be participating in the test programme by the autumn of 1971.

Notes: The VAK 191B was originally designed to meet an Italo-German requirement for a subsonic VTOL tactical reconnaissance fighter which was discarded as a result of changes in German strategy. With completion of the exploration of the flight envelope of the VAK 191B, the prototypes will be transferred by the manufacturer to the German Government for use as systems test vehicles for the Panavia multi-role combat aircraft (MRCA), evaluating avionic components and flight control elements.

VFW-FOKKER VAK 191B

Dimensions: Span, 20 ft 2½ in (6,16 m); length, 48 ft 3½ in (14,72 m); height, 14 ft 1 in (4,29 m); wing area, 134·5 sq ft (12,5 m²).

VFW-FOKKER VFW 614

Country of Origin: Federal Germany.

Type: Short-range commercial transport.

Power Plant: Two 7,510 (3 410 kg) Rolls-Royce/SNECMA M45H turbofans.

Performance: (Estimated) Max. speed, 457 mph (735 km/h) at 21,000 ft (6 400 m); max. cruise, 449 mph (722 km/h) at 25,000 ft (7 620 m); long-range cruise, 390 mph (627 km/h) at 25,000 ft (7 620 m); range with max. fuel, 1,145 mls (1 845 km), with max. payload, 390 mls (630 km); initial climb rate, 3,248 ft min (16,5 m/sec).

Weights: Operational empty, 26,896 lb (12 000 kg); max. take-off, 41,006 lb (18 600 kg).

Accommodation: Basic flight crew of two and alternative passenger configurations for 36, 40 or 44 seats in four-abreast rows.

Status: First of three prototypes scheduled to be rolled out in April 1971 and to commence its flight test programme in June. First deliveries scheduled for 1972.

Notes: The VFW 614 is being manufactured as a collaborative venture under the leadership of VFW-Fokker, participants including the Dutch Fokker-VFW concern and the Belgian SABCA and Fairey companies. The VFW 614 is intended as an ultra-short-haul DC-3 replacement, and an unconventional feature is its over-wing engine-pod installation. Emphasis has been placed on flexibility of operation in a wide variety of different environments and with a minimum of maintenance.

VFW-FOKKER VFW 614

Dimensions: Span, 70 ft 6½ in (21,50 m); length, 67 ft 7 in (20,60 m); height, 25 ft 8 in (7,84 m); wing area, 688·89 sq ft (64,00 m²).

VOUGHT A-7E CORSAIR II

Country of Origin: USA.
Type: Single-seat shipboard tactical fighter.
Power Plant: One 15,000 lb (6 804 kg) Allison TF41-A-2 (Rolls-Royce RB. 168-62 Spey) turbofan.
Performance: Max. speed without external stores, 699 mph (1 125 km/h) or Mach 0·92 at sea level, with 12 250-lb (113,4-kg) bombs, 633 mph (1 020 km/h) or Mach 0·87 at sea level; tactical radius with 12 250-lb (113,4-kg) bombs for hi-lo-hi mission at average cruise of 532 mph (856 km/h) with 1 hr on station, 512 mls (825 km); ferry range on internal fuel, 2,775 mls (4 465 km).
Weights: Empty equipped, 17,569 lb (7 969 kg); max. take-off, 42,000+ lb (19 050+ kg).
Armament: One 20-mm M-61A-1 rotary cannon with 1,000 rounds and (for short-range interdiction) maximum ordnance load of 20,000 lb (9 072 kg) distributed between eight external stores stations.
Status: A-7E first flown November 25, 1968, with production deliveries to US Navy following mid-1969. First 67 delivered with Pratt & Whitney TF30-P-8 turbofan. Planned procurement totals 618 aircraft.
Notes: A-7E is the shipboard equivalent of the USAF's A-7D (see 1970 edition). Preceded into service by A-7A (199 built) and A-7B (196 built) with 11,350 lb (5 150 kg) TF30-P-6 and 12,200 lb (5 534 kg) TF30-P-8 respectively. The A-7G is a proposed version for the Swiss Air Force with an uprated TF41-A-3 turbofan, and a supersonic version with a TF30-P-408 and afterburner has been proposed for USMC use.

VOUGHT A-7E CORSAIR II

Dimensions: Span, 38 ft 8¾ in (11,80 m); length, 46 ft 1½ in (14,06 m); height, 16 ft 0¾ in (4,90 m); wing area, 375 sq ft (34,83 m²).

YAKOVLEV YAK-28 (BREWER)

Country of Origin: USSR.

Type: Two-seat tactical strike and reconnaissance aircraft.

Power Plant: Two 10,140 lb (4 600 kg) dry and 13,670 lb (6 200 kg) reheat Tumansky RD-11 turbojets.

Performance: (Estimated) Max. speed without external stores, 720 mph (1 160 km/h) or Mach 0·95 at 1,000 ft (305 m), 730 mph (1 175 km/h) or Mach 1·1 at 39,370 ft (12 000 m); tactical radius with two 220 Imp gal (1 000 l) drop tanks for lo-lo-lo mission profile, 250 mls (400 km), for hi-lo-hi mission profile, 490 mls (790 km); max. range with drop tanks and auxiliary weapons-bay tank, 1,500–1,600 mls (2 415–2 575 km).

Weights: (Estimated) Normal take-off, 37,480 lb (17 000 kg); max. take-off, 41,890 lb (19 000 kg).

Armament: One 30-mm NR-30 cannon on starboard side of forward fuselage. Internal weapons bay believed to accommodate four 551-lb (250-kg) bombs, and bombs, ASMs or gunpods on two stores stations under wings.

Status: Flown in prototype form in 1960 with production deliveries to Soviet Air Forces commencing 1962–63.

Notes: The Yak-28 was developed as a successor to the Yak-26 Mangrove (two 5,732 lb/2 600 kg dry and 7,165 lb/3 250 kg reheat Tumansky RD-9s) with which it shares only a family resemblance. Developed in parallel with the Yak-28P (see pages 242–243), the basic Yak-28 originally featured a shorter fuselage and shorter engine nacelles, later production aircraft having a 2 ft 6 in (76 cm) lengthening forward of the wing (similar to Yak-28P) and 2 ft (61 cm) longer engine nacelles.

YAKOVLEV YAK-28 (BREWER)

Dimensions: (Estimated) Span, 44 ft 6 in (13,56 m); length (with probe), 75 ft 0 in (22,86 m), (without probe), 67 ft 0 in (20,42 m); height, 15 ft 0 in (4,57 m).

YAKOVLEV YAK-28P (FIREBAR)

Country of Origin: USSR.

Type: Two-seat all-weather interceptor fighter.

Power Plant: Two 10,140 lb (4 600 kg) dry and 13,670 lb (6 200 kg) reheat Tumansky RD-11 turbojets.

Performance: (Estimated) Max. speed without external stores, 760 mph (1 225 km/h) or Mach 1·15 at 39,370 ft (12 000 m), with two Anab AAMs, 695 mph (1 120 km/h) or Mach 1·05; normal cruise, 560 mph (900 km/h) or Mach 0·9; tactical radius for high-altitude patrol mission, 550 mls (885 km); initial climb, 28,000 ft/min (142,2 m/sec); service ceiling, 55,000 ft (16 765 m).

Weights: (Estimated) Normal take-off, 37,480 lb (17 000 kg); max. take-off, 40,785 lb (18 500 kg).

Armament: Standard armament comprises two Anab semi-active radar-homing AAMs carried by stores stations under wing. Some examples have been seen with four wing stores stations for two Anab AAMs and two infra-red homing Atoll AAMs.

Status: Flown in prototype form in 1960 with production deliveries commencing 1963–64.

Notes: The Yak-28P was developed in parallel with the Yak-28 tactical strike-recce aircraft, featuring a dielectric nose cone, tandem seating for the two crew members with windscreen (and twin-wheel forward member of "bicycle" undercarriage) about 2 ft 6 in (76 cm) further forward, and internal weapons bay deleted, this space presumably being occupied by fuel tankage. The Yak-28P is widely used by the Soviet Air Forces.

YAKOVLEV YAK-28P (FIREBAR)

Dimensions: (Estimated) Span, 44 ft 6 in (13,56 m); length (with probe), 75 ft 0 in (22,86 m), (without probe), 67 ft 0 in (20,42 m); height, 15 ft 0 in (4,57 m).

243

YAKOVLEV YAK-40 (CODLING)

Country of Origin: USSR.

Type: Short-range commercial feederliner.

Power Plant: Three 3,307 lb (1 500 kg) Ivchenko AI-25 turbofans.

Performance: Max. speed, 373 mph (600 km/h) at sea level, 466 mph (750 km/h) at 17,000 ft (5 180 m); max. cruise, 342 mph (550 km/h) at 19,685 ft (6 000 m); econ. cruise, 310 mph (500 km/h) at 32,810 ft (10 000 m); range with 5,070-lb (2 300-kg) payload at econ. cruise, 620 mls (1 000 km), with 3,140-lb (1 425-kg) payload and max. fuel, 920 mls (1 480 km); initial climb, 2,000 ft/min (10,16 m/sec); service ceiling at max. loaded weight, 38,715 ft (11 800 m).

Weights: Empty equipped, 18,916 lb (8 580 kg); max. take-off, 30,203 lb (13 700 kg).

Accommodation: Flight crew of two, and alternative arrangements for 24 or 27 passengers in three-abreast rows. High-density arrangement for up to 33 passengers, and business executive configurations for 8–10 passengers.

Status: First of five prototypes flown October 21, 1966, and first production deliveries (to *Aeroflot*) mid-1968. Some 270 delivered by beginning of 1971 when production rate was eight per month.

Notes: Development of a stretched version, the Yak-40M, with two 3 ft 3½ in (1,00 m) additional fuselage sections inserted fore and aft of the wing, and 3,850-lb (1 750-kg) AI-25 turbofans, was under development at beginning of 1971. The Yak-40M will accommodate 33–40 passengers.

YAKOVLEV YAK-40 (CODLING)

Dimensions: Span, 82 ft 0¼ in (25,00 m); length, 66 ft 9½ in (20,36 m); height, 21 ft 4 in (6,50 m); wing area, 753·473 sq ft (70 m²).

ZLIN 43-210

Country of Origin: Czechoslovakia.
Type: Light training and touring aircraft.
Power Plant: One 210 hp Avia M 337 six-cylinder inline inverted engine.
Performance: Max. speed, 143 mph (230 km/h) at sea level; max. cruise, 124 mph (200 km/h); max. range, 375 mls (610 km), with optional 12 Imp gal (55 l) wingtip tanks, 680 mls (1 100 km); initial climb, 650 ft/min (3,3 m/sec); service ceiling, 14,775 ft (4 500 m).
Weights: Empty equipped, 1,543 lb (700 kg); max. take-off, 2,775 lb (1 250 kg).
Accommodation: Four persons in side-by-side pairs with individual seats forward and bench-type seat at rear.
Status: First of two prototypes flown November 1968 and series production expected to commence late 1971 or early 1972.
Notes: The Z 43 shares extensive commonality of structural components with the side-by-side two-seat Z 42 (see 1969 edition) of which five prototypes had flown and a pre-series of 10 aircraft commenced by the beginning of 1971. The standard production version of the Z 43 is expected to have the M 337 engine, but plans have been announced for a version intended primarily for export to the West, the Z 43L-200 with a 200 hp Lycoming AIO-360 engine.

ZLIN 43-210

Dimensions: Span, 32 ft $0\frac{1}{4}$ in (9,76 m); length, 25 ft 5 in (7,75 m); height, 9 ft $6\frac{1}{2}$ in (2,91 m); wing area, 156·1 sq ft (14,5 m²).

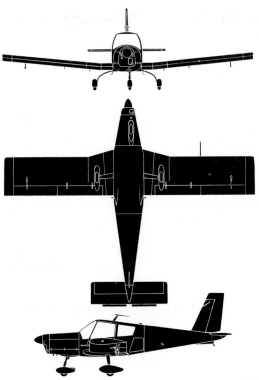

ZLIN 526L-200 SKYDEVIL

Country of Origin: Czechoslovakia.
Type: Tandem two-seat basic training aircraft.
Power Plant: One 200 hp Lycoming AIO-360-B1B four-cylinder horizontally-opposed engine.
Performance: Max. speed, 158 mph (255 km/h); cruise, 140 mph (225 km/h); max. range, 285 mls (460 km/h), with 15 Imp gal (68 l) auxiliary wingtip tanks, 440 mls (710 km/h); initial climb, 1,378 ft/min (7 m/sec); service ceiling, 22,300 ft (6 800 m).
Weights: Empty equipped, 1,485 lb (675 kg); max. take-off, 2,150 lb (975 kg).
Status: Prototype Z 526L flown August 27, 1969, with series production scheduled to commence during 1971.
Notes: The Z 526L is a Lycoming-engined derivative of the Z 526F powered by a 180 hp Avia M 137 six-cylinder inverted air-cooled engine, this being, in turn, a refinement of the basic Z 526 Trener-Master (see 1967 edition) powered by the Walter Minor 6-III of similar power. Production of the Z 526F is continuing, and a new clipped-wing aerobatic competition single-seat version, the Z 526AF, is being developed for the 1972 World Aerobatic Championship, this having a blown canopy and a span of 29 ft (8,84 m). Powered by the M 137 engine, the Z 526AF was scheduled to fly early 1971. Development of a further version of the basic design, the Z 626, is also being undertaken, and, embodying a number of refinements, is scheduled to fly in prototype form late in 1972. More than 1,500 examples of the various derivatives of the original Z 26 Trener have been built since 1947.

ZLIN 526L-200 SKYDEVIL

Dimensions: Span, 34 ft 9 in (10,60 m); length, 25 ft 1¼ in (7,65 m); height, 6 ft 9 in (2,06 m); wing area, 166·3 sq ft (15,45 m²).

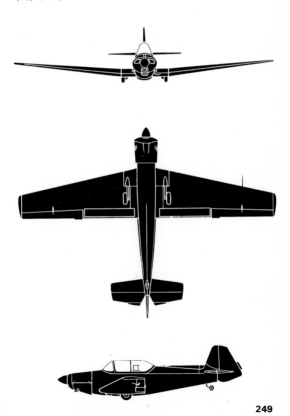

AÉROSPATIALE SA 318C ALOUETTE II

Country of Origin: France.
Type: Five-seat light utility helicopter.
Power Plant: One 523 shp Turboméca Astazou IIA turbo-shaft.
Performance: Max. speed, 127 mph (205 km/h) at sea level; max. cruise, 112 mph (180 km/h); max. inclined climb, 1,396 ft/min (7, 1 m/sec); hovering ceiling (in ground effect), 5,085 ft (1 550 m), (out of ground effect), 2,950 ft (900 m); range with max. fuel, 447 mls (720 km), with max. payload, 62 mls (100 km).
Weights: Empty, 1,961 lb (890 kg); max. take-off, 3,630 lb (1 650 kg).
Dimensions: Rotor diam, 33 ft 5⅝ in (10,20 m); fuselage length, 31 ft 11¾ in (9,75 m).
Notes: The SA 318C has been developed from the SE 313B Alouette II (see 1967 edition) which it has supplanted in production. The earlier model differed primarily in having an Artouste turboshaft, and 923 examples were built. The Astazou offers a 25 per cent improvement in fuel consumption and, together with other design changes, has provided the SA 318C version of the Alouette II with performance improvements and a 375-lb (170-kg) increase in payload. The SA 315 is a version of the Alouette II with an Artouste IIB and mechanical systems of the Alouette III certificated in 1970.

AÉROSPATIALE SA 319A ALOUETTE III

Country of Origin: France.

Type: Seven-seat light utility helicopter.

Power Plant: One 789 shp Turboméca Astazou XIV turboshaft.

Performance: Max. speed, 137 mph (220 km/h) at sea level; max. cruise, 122 mph (197 km/h); max. inclined climb, 853 ft/min (4,32 m/sec); hovering ceiling (in ground effect), 5,740 ft (1 750 m); range with six passengers, 375 mls (605 km).

Weights: Empty, 2,403 lb (1 090 kg); max. take-off, 4,960 lb (2 250 kg).

Dimensions: Rotor diam, 36 ft 1$\frac{3}{4}$ in (11,02 m); fuselage length, 32 ft 10$\frac{3}{4}$ in (10,03 m).

Notes: The SA 319 is an Astazou-powered derivative of the Artouste-powered SA 316 Alouette III. All Alouette IIIs built prior to 1970 had the Artouste turboshaft and are now designated SA316A, the 1970 production model with the Artouste IIIB of 858 shp derated to 543 shp being the SA 316B, and the 1971 model with the Artouste IIID being the SA 316C. The last-mentioned version is manufactured in parallel with the SA 319A, deliveries of which began late in 1970, and the SA 319B with the Astazou XVI will be introduced in 1971. Total of 962 Alouette IIIs sold by the beginning of 1971, and licence production being undertaken in India and Switzerland, and to commence in Rumania.

AÉROSPATIALE SA 321 SUPER FRELON

Country of Origin: France.

Type: Medium transport and multi-purpose helicopter.

Power Plant: Three 1,550 shp Turboméca Turmo III C6 turboshafts.

Performance: Max. speed, 149 mph (240 km/h) at sea level; max. cruise, 143 mph (230 km/h); max. inclined climb, 1,495 ft/min (7,6 m/sec); hovering ceiling (in ground effect), 7,380 ft (2 250 m), (out of ground effect), 1,804 ft (550 m); range with 5,511-lb (2 500-kg) payload and 20 min reserves, 404 mls (650 km).

Weights: Empty, 14,420 lb (6 540 kg); max. take-off, 27,557 lb (12 500 kg).

Dimensions: Rotor diam, 62 ft 0 in (18,90 m); fuselage length, 63 ft 7¾ in (19,40 m).

Notes: Several versions of the Super Frelon (Super Hornet) have been manufactured, including the SA 321G amphibious ASW model for the *Aéronavale* with Sylph radars in outrigger floats, dunking sonar and up to four torpedoes and other ASW stores, the non-amphibious military transport SA 321K (Israel) and SA 321L (South Africa) capable of carrying 27–30 troops or 8,818–9,920 lb (4 000–4 500 kg) cargo (the SA 321L being illustrated), and the commercial SA 321F (34–37 passenger airliner) and SA 321J heavy-duty utility models.

AÉROSPATIALE SA 330 PUMA

Country of Origin: France.
Type: Medium transport helicopter.
Power Plant: Two 1,320 shp Turboméca Turmo III C4 turbo-shafts.
Performance: Max. Speed, 174 mph (280 km/h) at sea level; max. cruise, 165 mph (265 km/h); max. inclined climb, 1,400 ft/min (7,1 m/sec); hovering ceiling (in ground effect), 9,186 ft (2 800 m), (out of ground effect), 6,233 ft (1 900 m); max. range, 390 mls (630 km).
Weights: Empty, 7,561 lb (3 430 kg); max. take-off, 14,110 (6 400 kg).
Dimensions: Rotor diam, 49 ft 2½ on (15,00 m), fuselage length, 46 ft 1½ in (14,06 m).
Notes: The Puma is being built under a joint production agreement between Aérospatiale and Westland, the first to be assembled by the latter concern flying on November 25, 1970. The Puma can accommodate 16–20 troops or up to 5,511 lb (2 500 kg) of cargo, and 40 are being delivered to the RAF for the assault role, 88 having been ordered by French Army Aviation. The Puma has been supplied to the Portuguese, South African, Congolese, Algerian, and Ivory Coast air arms, and a commercial version, the SA 330F with 1,385 shp Turmo IVA turboshafts, is under development, this carrying 15–17 passengers over 217 mls (350 km).

AÉROSPATIALE SA 341 GAZELLE

Country of Origin: France.
Type: Five-seat light utility helicopter.
Power Plant: One 592 shp Turboméca Astazou IIIN turbo-shaft.
Performance: Max. speed, 165 mph (265 km/h) at sea level; max. cruise, 149 mph (240 km/h); max. inclined climb rate, 1,214 ft/min (6,16 m/sec); hovering ceiling (in ground effect), 10,170 ft (3 100 m), (out of ground effect), 8,530 ft (2 600 m); max. range, 403 mls (650 km).
Weights: Empty, 1,873 lb (850 kg); max. take-off, 3,747 lb (1 700 kg).
Dimensions: Rotor diam, 34 ft 5½ in (10,50 m); fuselage length, 31 ft 2¾ in (9,52 m).
Notes: Intended as a successor to the Alouette II, the Gazelle is being built under a joint production agreement between Aérospatiale and Westland. Two prototypes and four pre-production Gazelles have flown, and series production is scheduled to commence late in 1971. The Gazelle is to be operated in the LOH (Light Observation Helicopter) role by both the French and British armed forces, and it is antici-pated that these will respectively purchase some 170 and 250 Gazelles during the first half of the decade. Licence pro-duction was being considered in Australia and Yugoslavia during early 1971.

AIRMARK WALLIS WA-117

Country of Origin: United Kingdom.

Type: Single-seat ultra-light autogyro.

Power Plant: One 100 hp Rolls-Royce Continental 0-200-B four-cylinder horizontally-opposed engine.

Performance: Max. speed, 120 mph (193 km/h) at sea level; max. cruise, 90 mph (145 km/h); max. inclined climb, 1,000 ft/min (5,08 m/sec); max. range, 170 mls (273 km) at 70 mph (113 km/h).

Weights: Empty, 375 lb (170 kg); max. take-off, 700 lb (317 kg).

Dimensions: Rotor diam, 20 ft 0 in (6,09 m); fuselage length, 12 ft 0 in (3,66 m).

Notes: The WA-117, which is to be manufactured and marketed by Airmark Limited during 1971, is a progressive development of the basic Wallis autogyro, employing proven features of the WA-116 Agile (see 1967 edition) and a more powerful engine. Flight trials of an experimental test vehicle for the WA-117 began in March 1965, a pre-production prototype flying in May 1967, and in its production form the WA-117 will be available with a fully-enclosed cockpit and other design refinements. A further derivative of the basic design is the WA-118 Meteorite of which two prototypes have been built, these being powered by a suitably modified Italian Meteor Alfa Engine rated at 120 hp.

BELL MODEL 204B (IROQUOIS)

Country of Origin: USA.

Type: Ten-seat utility helicopter.

Power Plant: One 1,100 shp Lycoming T5311A turboshaft.

Performance: (At 8,500 lb/3 855 kg) Max. speed, 120 mph (193 km/h) at sea level; max. cruise, 110 mph (177 km/h); max. inclined climb, 1,400 ft/min (7,1 m/sec); hovering ceiling (in ground effect), 10,000 ft (3 050 m), (out of ground effect), 4,500 ft (1 370 m); max. range, 392 mls (630 km).

Weights: Empty, 4,600 lb (2 086 kg); max. take-off, 9,500 lb (4 309 kg).

Dimensions: Rotor diam, 48 ft 0 in (14,63 m); fuselage length 40 ft 4⅞ in (12,31 m).

Notes: Licence manufacture of Model 204B undertaken in Italy by Agusta (as AB 204B) and in Japan by Fuji. Variants for US forces include UH-1B and -1C (two crew and seven troops) for US Army, UH-1E (assault support equivalent of of the UH-1C) for the USMC, the UH-1F (missile-site support model with a 1,272 shp General Electric T58-GE-3) and TH-1F (trainer) for the USAF, and the HH-1K (sea-rescue version of the UH-1E with a 1,400 shp Lycoming T53 L-13), TH-1L Seawolf (T53-L-13-powered trainer), and the UH-1L (utility version of the TH-1L) for the US Navy. The AB-204B may have the Gnome H.1200 or T58-GE-3 turboshaft.

BELL MODEL 205A (IROQUOIS)

Country of Origin: USA.

Type: Fifteen-seat utility helicopter.

Power Plant: One 1,400 shp Lycoming T5313A turboshaft.

Performance: (At 9,500 lb/4 309 kg) Max. speed, 127 mph (204 km/h) at sea level; max. cruise, 111 mph (179 km/h) at 8,000 ft (2 440 m); max. inclined climb, 1,680 ft/min (8,53 m/sec); hovering ceiling (in ground effect), 10,400 ft (3 170 m), (out of ground effect), 6,000 ft (1 830 m); range, 344 mls (553 km) at 8,000 ft (2 440 m).

Weights: Empty equipped, 5,082 lb (2 305 kg); normal take-off, 9,500 lb (4 309 kg).

Dimensions: Rotor diam, 48 ft 0 in (14,63 m); fuselage length, 41 ft 6 in (12,65 m).

Notes: The Model 205A is basically similar to the Model 204B but introduces a longer fuselage with increased cabin space. It is produced under licence in Italy by Agusta as the AB 205, and is assembled under licence in Formosa (Taiwan). The initial version for the US Army, the UH-1D, has a 1,100 shp T53-L-11 turboshaft. This model is being manufactured under licence in Federal Germany. The UH-1D has been succeeded in production for the US Army by the UH-1H with a 1,400 shp T53-L-13 turboshaft, and a similar helicopter for the Mobile Command of the Canadian Armed Forces is designated CUH-1H.

BELL MODEL 206A JETRANGER

Country of Origin: USA.

Type: Five-seat light utility helicopter.

Power Plant: One 317 shp Allison 250-C18A turboshaft.

Performance: Max. speed, 150 mph (241 km/h) at sea level; max. cruise, 131 mph (211 km/h); max. inclined climb at 3,000 lb (1 360 kg), 1,450 ft/min (7,36 m/sec); hovering ceiling (in ground effect), 7,900 ft (2 410 m), (out of ground effect), 3,350 ft (1 020 m); max. range at 2,100 lb (953 kg), 460 mls (740 km), at 3,000 lb (1 360 kg), 392 mls (630 km).

Weights: Empty, 1,425 lb (646 kg); max. take-off, 3,000 lb (1 360 kg).

Dimensions: Rotor diam, 33 ft 4 in (10,16 m); fuselage length, 31 ft 2 in (9,50 m).

Notes: The Model 206A JetRanger is manufactured in both commercial and military versions. Forty have been delivered to the US Navy for the training role as the TH-57A Sea-Ranger, and a light observation version is being produced for the US Army as the OH-58A Kiowa. The latter differs from the basic Model 206A in having a larger main rotor of 35 ft 4 in (10,77 m) diameter, a fuselage of 32 ft 3½ in (9,84 m) length, and other changes. A version of the JetRanger basically similar to the OH-58A is built in Italy by Agusta as the AB 206A-1, and has been exported in some numbers for both civil and military use.

BELL MODEL 209 HUEYCOBRA

Country of Origin: USA.

Type: Two-seat attack helicopter.

Power Plant: (AH-1G) One 1,400 shp Lycoming T53-L-13 turboshaft.

Performance: (AH-1G) Max. speed, 219 mph (352 km/h) at sea level; max. inclined climb, 1,580 ft/min (8 m/sec); hovering ceiling (in ground effect), 9,900 ft (3 015 m); max. range, 387 mls (622 km) at sea level.

Weights: Operational empty, 6,096 lb (2 765 kg); max. take-off, 9,500 lb (4 309 kg).

Dimensions: Rotor diam, 44 ft 0 in (13,41 m); fuselage length, 44 ft 5 in (13,54 m).

Notes: The Model 209 is a development of the UH-1C version of the Model 204B (see page 256) specifically for armed missions. The version for the US Army, the AH-1G (described and illustrated above), has two 7,62-mm Miniguns with 4,000 rpg or two 40-mm grenade launchers with 300 rpg in a forward barbette, and four external stores stations for rockets or gun pods under the stub-wings. The variant for the USMC, the AH-1J SeaCobra, differs from the AH-1G in having a 1,800 shp Pratt & Whitney T400-CP-400 coupled free-turbine turboshaft, a three-barrel 20-mm cannon in the chin barbette, a strengthened tail rotor pylon, and a maximum take-off weight of 10,000 lb (4 535 kg). SeaCobra deliveries commenced mid-1970.

BELL MODEL 212 TWIN TWO-TWELVE

Country of Origin: USA.
Type: Fifteen-seat utility helicopter.
Power Plant: One 1,800 shp Pratt & Whitney PT6T-3 coupled turboshaft.
Performance: Max. speed, 121 mph (194 km/h) at sea level; max. inclined climb at 10,000 lb (4 535 kg), 1,460 ft/min (7,4 m/sec); hovering ceiling (in ground effect), 17,100 ft (5 212 m), (out of ground effect), 9,900 ft (3 020 m); max. range, 296 mls (476 km) at sea level.
Weights: Empty, 5,500 lb (2 495 kg); max. take-off, 10,000 lb (4 535 kg).
Dimensions: Rotor diam, 48 ft 2½ in (14,69 m); fuselage length, 42 ft 10¾ in (13,07 m).
Notes: The Model 212 is based on the Model 205 (see page 257) from which it differs primarily in having a twin-engined power plant (two turboshaft engines coupled to a combining gearbox with a single output shaft), and both commercial and military versions are being produced. A model for the Canadian Armed Forces is designated CUH-1N, and an essentially similar variant of the Model 212, the UH-1N, is being supplied to the USAF, the USN, and the USMC. All versions of the Model 212 can carry an external load of 4,400 lb (1 814 kg), and can maintain cruise performance on one engine component at maximum gross weight.

BOEING-VERTOL MODEL 107-II

Country of Origin: USA.

Type: Medium transport helicopter.

Power Plant: Two 1,500 shp General Electric T58-GE-5 turboshafts.

Performance: (At 20,800 lb/9 434 kg) Max. speed, 139 mph (224 km/h); max. inclined climb, 1,920 ft/min (9,75 m/sec); hovering ceiling (in ground effect), 10,000 ft (3 048 m), (out of ground effect), 7,100 ft (2 165 m); range with 2,400 lb (1 088 kg) payload and 30 min reserves, 633 mls (1 020 km).

Weights: Empty equipped, 11,585 lb (5 240 kg); max. take-off, 21,400 lb (9 706 kg).

Dimensions: Rotor diam (each), 50 ft 0 in (15,24 m); fuselage length, 44 ft 10 in (13,66 m).

Notes: The Model 107-II has been in continuous production for military and civil tasks for 10 years, and is licence-manufactured by Kawasaki in Japan. The specification relates to the latest basic utility model, and a Kawasaki-built example (KV-107-II-3) of the Japanese Maritime Self-Defence Force is illustrated. Versions supplied to the US services comprise the CH-46A (1,250 shp T58-GE-8Bs) and CH-46D (1,400 shp T58-GE-10s) Sea Knight assault transports for the USMC, and the similarly-powered UH-46A and UH-46D Sea Knight utility models for the US Navy. The Model 107-II accommodates three crew and 25 passengers.

BOEING-VERTOL MODEL 114

Country of Origin: USA.

Type: Medium transport helicopter.

Power Plant: (CH-47C) Two 3,750 shp Lycoming T55-L-11 turboshafts.

Performance: (CH-47C at 33,000 lb/14 969 kg) Max. speed, 190 mph (306 km/h) at sea level; average cruise, 158 mph (254 km/h); max. inclined climb, 2,880 ft/min (14,63 m/sec); hovering ceiling (out of ground effect), 14,750 ft (4 495 m); mission radius, 115 mls (185 km).

Weights: Empty, 20,378 lb (9 243); max. take-off, 46,000 lb (20 865 kg).

Dimensions: Rotor diam (each), 60 ft 0 in (18,29 m); fuselage length, 51 ft 0 in (15,54 m).

Notes: The Model 114 is the standard medium transport helicopter of the US Army, and is operated by that service under the designation CH-47 Chinook. The initial production model, the CH-47A, was powered by 2,200 shp T55-L-5 or 2,650 shp T55-L-7 turboshafts. This was succeeded by the CH-47B (illustrated) with 2,850 shp T55-L-7C engines, redesigned rotor blades and other modifications, and this, in turn, gave place to the current CH-47C with more powerful engines, strengthened transmissions, and increased fuel in Italy by Elicotteri Meridionali, and 12 helicopters of this type have been ordered for the RAAF.

CAMPBELL CRICKET

Country of Origin: United Kingdom.

Type: Single-seat ultra-light autogyro.

Power Plant: One 75 hp modified Volkswagen 1,600 cc engine.

Performance: Max. speed, 80 mph (129 km/h) at sea level; max. cruise, 65 mph (105 km/h); econ. cruise, 60 mph (97 km/h); max. inclined climb, 740 ft/min (3,76 m/sec); service ceiling, 11,000 ft (3 353 m); range, 253 mls (407 km).

Weights: Empty (excluding rotors), 295 lb (133,5 kg); max. take-off, 650 lb (294,5 kg).

Dimensions: Rotor diam, 21 ft 9 in (6,63 m); fuselage length, 11 ft 3 in (3,43 m).

Notes: Designed and developed by Campbell Aircraft Limited, which previously manufactured Bensen Gyro-Gliders and Gyro-Copters under licence, the Cricket was flown for the first time in July 1969, series production of this ultra-light autogyro commencing shortly afterwards. The Cricket can take-off within 105 ft (32 m), attain an altitude of 50 ft (15 m) within 330 ft (101 m), and land from 50 ft (15 m) within 50 ft (15 m), the landing run being only 3 ft (1 m). The pilot is accommodated in a glass-fibre nacelle, and the Cricket is claimed to be suitable for a variety of tasks, including aerial photographic work. Radio equipment is optional.

CIERVA ROTORCRAFT CR.LTH-1

Country of Origin: United Kingdom.
Type: Five-seat light utility helicopter.
Power Plant: Two 205 shp Continental IO-360 six-cylinder horizontally-opposed engines.
Performance: (At 3,250 lb/1 474 kg) Max. speed, 125 mph (201 km/h) at sea level; max. cruise, 120 mph (193 km/h); max. inclined climb, 1,400 ft/min (7,1 m/sec); hovering ceiling (out of ground effect), 7,500 ft (2 286 m); range with 30 min reserves, 250 mls (402 km).
Weights: Empty, 1,860 lb (844 kg); max. take-off, 3,250 lb (1 474 kg).
Dimensions: Rotor diam, 32 ft 0 in (9,75 m); fuselage length, 26 ft 4 in (8,026 m).
Notes: The CR.LTH-1 light utility helicopter has been developed by Cierva Rotorcraft Limited, formerly the Cierva Autogiro Company, to the designs of Servotec Limited, and the first of two prototypes was flown on August 18, 1969. The second prototype is illustrated above, and current plans call for the completion of the first production model during 1972 with deliveries commencing in 1973. The production model can be powered by either the Continental IO-360 or the Lycoming HIO-360 which drive coaxial contra-rotating rotors, and emphasis is placed on low initial cost and operational economy.

FAIRCHILD HILLER FH-1100

Country of Origin: USA.

Type: Five-seat light utility helicopter.

Power Plant: One 317 shp Allison 250-C18 turboshaft.

Performance: Max. speed, 127 mph (204 km/h) at sea level; econ. cruise, 122 mph (196 km/h); max. inclined climb, 1,600 ft/min (8,1 m/sec); hovering ceiling (in ground effect), 13,400 ft (4 085 m), (out of ground effect), 8,400 ft (2 560 m); range with max. payload, 348 mls (560 km).

Weights: Empty, 1,396 lb (633 kg); max. take-off, 2,750 lb (1 247 kg).

Dimensions: Rotor diam, 35 ft 4¾ in (10,79 m); fuselage length, 29 ft 9½ in (9,08 m).

Notes: The FH-1100 is a refined derivative of the OH-5A which was runner-up in the US Army's first light observation helicopter contest, and the first production model was completed in June 1966. The FH-1100 has since been manufactured in some numbers, primarily for civil duties, and an aeromedical version provides accommodation for two casualty stretchers and a medical attendant. The FH-1100 serves with the Thai Royal Border Police, and is suitable for a variety of military roles. Provision can be made for a wide range of weapons, including torpedoes, depth charges, minigun pods, and rocket launchers, and the FH-1100 has been flown in level flight at 160 mph (257 km/h).

HUGHES MODEL 300

Country of Origin: USA.

Type: Three-seat light utility helicopter.

Power Plant: (Model 300C) One 190 shp Lycoming HIO-360-D1A four-cylinder horizontally-opposed engine.

Performance: (Model 300C) Max. speed, 105 mph (169 km/h); max. cruise, 100 mph (161 km/h) at 5,000 ft (1 525 m); max. inclined climb, 1,100 ft/min (5,08 m/sec); hovering ceiling (in ground effect), 7,600 ft (2 316 m), (out of ground effect), 5,200 ft (1 585 m); max. range, 255 mls (410 km).

Weights: Empty, 1,025 lb (465 kg); max. take-off, 1,900 lb (861 kg).

Dimensions: Rotor diam, 26 ft 10 in (8,18 m); fuselage length, 23 ft 1 in (7,03 m).

Notes: Originally developed as the Model 269B, the Model 300 has been in continuous production since 1963, and 792 examples of this light helicopter have been supplied to the US Army for the primary training role as the TH-55A. The current production version, the Model 300C described by the specification, differs from the basic Model 300 (which was powered by a 180 hp Lycoming HIO-360-A1A) in having a more powerful engine, main and tail rotors of increased diameter, and structural changes including a lengthened tail boom and a taller rotor mast. Deliveries of the Model 300C commenced in 1970.

HUGHES MODEL 500

Country of Origin: USA.

Type: Six-seat light utility helicopter.

Power Plant: One 317 shp Allison 250-C18A turboshaft.

Performance: Max. speed, 152 mph (244 km/h) at 1,000 ft (305 m); range cruise, 138 mph (222 km/h) at sea level; max. inclined climb, 1,700 ft/min (8,64 m/sec); hovering ceiling (in ground effect), 8,200 ft (2 500 m), (out of ground effect), 5,300 ft (1 615 m); max. range, 377 mls (589 km) at 4,000 ft (1 220 m).

Weights: Empty, 1,086 lb (492 kg); max. take-off, 2,550 lb (1 157 kg).

Dimensions: Rotor diam, 26 ft 4 in (8,03 m); fuselage length, 23 ft 0 in (7,01 m).

Notes: The Model 500 (also known by the engineering designation Model 369) is being manufactured for both commercial and foreign military use, the military configuration being known as the Model 500M. Both Models 500 and 500M have been assembled in Italy by Nardi which will begin licence manufacture during 1971, and licence manufacture is also being undertaken by Kawasaki in Japan. The current Model 500 is essentially similar to the OH-6A Cayuse light observation helicopter for the US Army, but its turboshaft is only derated to 278 shp (as compared with 252 shp for the Allison T63-A-5A of the OH-6A), and internal volume and fuel capacity are increased.

KAMAN HH-2 SEASPRITE

Country of Origin: USA.

Type: All-weather search and rescue helicopter.

Power Plant: Two 1,250 shp General Electric T58-GE-8B turboshafts.

Performance: (HH-2D) Max. speed, 168 mph (270 km/h) at sea level; normal cruise, 152 mph (245 km/h); max. inclined climb, 2,540 ft/min (12,9 m/sec); hovering ceiling (in ground effect), 16,900 ft (5 150 m), (out of ground effect), 14,100 ft (4 300 m); max. range, 425 mls (685 km).

Weights: (HH-2D) Empty, 7,500 lb (3 401 kg); normal take-off, 10,187 lb (4 620 kg); max. overload, 12,500 lb (5 670 kg).

Dimensions: Rotor diam, 44 ft 0 in (13,41 m); fuselage length, 37 ft 8 in (11,48 m).

Notes: The HH-2C and HH-2D are specialised search and rescue conversions of the single-engined UH-2A and -2B multi-role versions of the Seasprite (see 1966 edition), and, like the UH-2C (see 1969 edition), are modified to twin-engined configuration. The HH-2C is an armed and armoured model with a chin-mounted Minigun barbette and waist-mounted machine guns, and the HH-2D is similar but lacks armour and armament. The HH-2D differs from the UH-2C (illustrated) in having a four-bladed tail rotor, dual main-wheels, and uprated transmission. One hundred and ninety UH-2A and -2B Seasprites originally built.

KAMOV KA-25 (HORMONE)

Country of Origin: USSR.

Type: Shipboard anti-submarine warfare helicopter.

Power Plant: Two 900 shp Glushenkov GTD-3 turboshafts.

Performance: (Ka-25K) Max. speed, 137 mph (220 km/h); normal cruise, 121 mph (195 km/h); range with max. payload, 248 mls (400 km), with max. fuel, 404 mls (650 km); service ceiling, 10,670 ft (3 500 m).

Weights: (Ka-25K) Empty, 9,259 lb (4 200 kg); normal take-off, 15,653 lb (7 100 kg); max. take-off, 16,094 lb (7 300 kg).

Dimensions: Rotor diam (each), 51 ft 7$\frac{1}{2}$ in (15,74 m); fuselage length, 34 ft 3 in (10,44 m).

Notes: Developed to meet a requirement for a shipboard ASW helicopter, the Ka-25 was initially flown in prototype form in 1961, and was subsequently developed for both military and civil roles, the civil version, the Ka-25K (see 1970 edition), being flown in prototype form in 1965. The ASW Ka-25, which serves aboard the helicopter carriers *Moskva* and *Leningrad*, and the Ka-25K possess the same power plant, transmission system, and coaxial contra-rotating rotors, but the latter has a slightly shorter fuselage (32 ft 3 in/9,83 m), and aft-facing glazed gondola beneath the nose to accommodate a winch operator, and smaller vertical tail surfaces. The ASW Ka-25 is equipped with inflatable pontoons.

KAMOV KA-26 (HOODLUM)

Country of Origin: USSR.
Type: Light utility helicopter.
Power Plant: Two 325 shp Vedeneev M-14V-26 air-cooled radial engines.
Performance: Max. speed, 106 mph (170 km/h); max. cruise, 93 mph (150 km/h); econ. cruise, 56 mph (90 km/h) at 9,840 ft (3 000 m); hovering ceiling at 6,615 lb (3 000 kg) (in ground effect), 4,265 ft (1 300 m), (out of ground effect), 2,625 ft (800 m); range with seven passengers and 30 min reserves, 248 mls (400 km).
Weights: Empty (stripped), 4,300 lb (1 950 kg), (with passenger pod), 4,630 lb (2 100 kg); max. take-off, 7,165 lb (3 250 kg).
Dimensions: Rotor diam (each), 42 ft 8 in (13,00 m); fuselage length, 25 ft 5 in (7,75 m).
Notes: Flown for the first time in 1965, and placed in large-scale production during the following year, the Ka-26 was designed from the outset to carry interchangeable pods for freight or passengers, a chemical hopper with spraybars or dust-spreader, an open freight platform, or a hook for slung loads. The passenger-carrying pod (see fitted above) can accommodate up to six passengers, and in the aeromedical role the Ka-26 can carry two casualty stretchers, two seated casualties and a medical attendant.

MBB BO 105

Country of Origin: Federal Germany.
Type: Five/six-seat light utility helicopter.
Power Plant: Two 375 shp MTU 6022-701-A3 turboshafts.
Performance: (At 4,410 lb/2 000 kg) Max. speed, 155 mph (250 km/h) at sea level; max. cruise, 143 mph (230 km/h); max. inclined climb, 2,065 ft/min (6,29 m/sec); hovering ceiling (in ground effect), 15,090 ft (4 600 m), (out of ground effect), 11,480 ft (3 500 m); normal range, 440 mls (710 km) at 6,560 ft (2 000 m).
Weights: Empty, 2,360 lb (1 070 kg); normal take-off, 4,410 lb (2 000 kg); overload take-off, 5,070 lb (2 300 kg).
Dimensions: Rotor diam, 32 ft 1¾ in (9,80 m); fuselage length, 28 ft 0½ in (8,55 m).
Notes: The BO 105 features a rigid unarticulated main rotor with folding glass-fibre reinforced plastic blades, and the decision to initiate series production at the Siebelwerke-ATG subsidiary of MBB (Messerschmitt-Bölkow-Blohm) was taken in October 1970. Three prototypes and four pre-production BO 105s have been built, and production deliveries are to commence in 1971, Allison 250-C18 or -C20 turboshafts being offered as alternatives to the MTU turboshaft installed as standard. Boeing Vertol has acquired US manufacturing rights of the BO 105, and, during 1970, was offering this type to the US Navy.

MIL MI-2 (HOPLITE)

Country of Origin: USSR.

Type: Light general-purpose helicopter.

Power Plant: Two 437 shp Izotov GTD-350 turboshafts.

Performance: Max. speed, 130 mph (210 km/h) at 1,640 ft (500 m); max. cruise, 124 mph (200 km/h); econ. cruise, 118 mph (190 km/h); max. inclined climb, 885 ft/min (4,5 m/sec); hovering ceiling (in ground effect), 6,550 ft (2 000 m), (out of ground effect), 3,275 ft (1 000 m); range with max. payload and 5% reserves, 105 mls (170 km), with max. fuel and 30 min reserves, 360 mls (580 km).

Weights: Operational empty, 5,180 lb (2 350 kg); normal take-off, 7,826 lb (3 550 kg); overload take-off, 8,157 lb (3 700 kg).

Dimensions: Rotor diam, 47 ft 6¾ in (14,50 m); fuselage length, 37 ft 4¾ in (11,40 m).

Notes: After completion of prototype development in the Soviet Union, production and marketing of the Mi-2 were transferred to Poland where manufacture of this helicopter (at the WSK-Swidnik) has been undertaken since 1966. The Mi-2 has been built in large numbers for both civil and military tasks, and has been exported widely. Accommodation may be provided for a single pilot and six to eight passengers or up to 1,543 lb (700 kg) of freight. Four casualty stretchers and a medical attendant can be carried.

MIL MI-6 (HOOK)

Country of Origin: USSR.

Type: Heavy transport helicopter.

Power Plant: Two 5,500 shp Soloviev D-25V turboshafts.

Performance: (At 93,700 lb/42 500 kg) Max. speed, 186 mph (300 km/h); max. cruise, 155 mph (250 km/h); service ceiling, 14,750 ft (4 500 m); range with 17,640-lb (8 000-kg) payload, 385 mls (620 km), with 9,920-lb (4 500-kg) payload and external tanks, 620 mls (1 000 km).

Weights: Empty, 60,055 lb (27 240 kg); normal take-off, 89,285 lb (40 500 kg); max. take-off (for VTO), 93,700 lb (42 500 kg).

Dimensions: Rotor diam, 114 ft 10 in (35,00 m); fuselage length, 108 ft 9½ in (33,16 m).

Notes: First flown in 1957, the Mi-6 has been built in very large numbers for both civil and military roles. With a crew of five, the Mi-6 can accommodate 65 passengers or 41 casualty stretchers and two medical attendants, and clam-shell-type doors and folding ramps facilitate the loading of vehicles and bulky freight. Two heavy flying-crane helicopters have been evolved from the Mi-6, the Mi-10 (see 1966 edition) flown in 1961 and the Mi-10K (see 1970 edition) flown in 1965, these being almost identical to the Mi-6 above the line of the cabin. The Mi-6 has been supplied to the armed forces of North Vietnam, UAR and Indonesia.

MIL MI-8 (HIP)

Country of Origin: USSR.

Type: General-purpose transport helicopter.

Power Plant: Two 1,500 shp Izotov TB-2-117A turboshafts.

Performance: (At 24,470 lb/11 100 kg) Max. speed, 155 mph (250 km/h); max. cruise, 140 mph (225 km/h); hovering ceiling (in ground effect), 5,900 ft (1 800 m), (out of ground effect), 2,625 ft (800 m); service ceiling, 14,760 ft (4 500 m); range with 6,615 lb (3 000 kg) of freight, 264 mls (425 km).

Weights: Empty (cargo), 15,787 lb (7 171 kg), (passenger), 16,352 lb (7 417 kg); normal take-off, 24,470 lb (11 100 kg); max. take-off (for VTO), 26,455 lb (12 000 kg).

Dimensions: Rotor diam, 69 ft 10¼ in (21,29 m); fuselage length, 59 ft 7⅛ in (18,17 m).

Notes: The Mi-8 has been in continuous production since 1964 for both civil and military tasks. The standard commercial passenger version has a basic flight crew of two or three and 28 four-abreast seats, and the aeromedical version accommodates 12 casualty stretchers and a medical attendant. As a freighter the Mi-8 will carry up to 8,818 lb (4 000 kg) of cargo, and military tasks include assault transport, search and rescue, and anti-submarine warfare. The Mi-8 is now operated by several Warsaw Pact air forces, serving primarily in the support transport role.

MIL MI-12 (HOMER)

Country of Origin: USSR.

Type: Heavy transport helicopter.

Power Plant: Four 6,500 shp Soloviev D-25 turboshafts.

Performance: (Estimated) Max. speed, 180 mph (290 km/h); max. cruise, 160 mph (267 km/h); max. inclined climb with 68,410 lb (31 035 kg) payload, 590 ft/min (3,0 m/sec); max. ferry range, 3,100 mls (4 990 km).

Weights: Max. take-off, 198,000–202,000 lb (89 800– 91 630 kg).

Dimensions: (Estimated) Rotor diam (each), 115 ft 0 in (34,00 m).

Notes: The Mi-12 is currently the world's largest helicopter, and the first prototype reportedly commenced its flight test programme in the autumn of 1968. The Mi-12 employs the dynamic components of the Mi-6 (see page 273), being, in effect, two Mi-6 power units, main transmissions and main rotors mounted side-by-side at the tips of braced wings spanning some 240 ft (73,00 m) and married to a fuselage of entirely new design. The Mi-12 has reportedly progressed no further than prototype testing at the beginning of 1971, but is claimed to be capable of accommodating 175–250 passengers in its definitive commercial form, although its future role would appear to be primarily military. The Mi-12 has established several payload-to-height records.

SIKORSKY S-61A

Country of Origin: USA.
Type: Amphibious transport and rescue helicopter.
Power Plant: (S-61A-4) Two 1,500 shp General Electric
T58-GE-5 turboshafts.
Performance: (At 20,500 lb/9 300 kg) Max. speed, 153
mph (248 km/h); range cruise, 126 mph (203 km/h); max.
inclined climb, 2,200 ft/min (11,17 m/sec); hovering ceiling
(in ground effect), 8,600 ft (2 820 m); range with max. fuel
and 10 % reserves, 525 mls (845 km).
Weights: Empty, 9,763 lb (4 428 kg); normal take-off,
20,500 lb (9 300 kg); max., 21,500 lb (9 750 kg).
Dimensions: Rotor diam, 62 ft 0 in (18,90 m); fuselage
length, 54 ft 9 in (16,69 m).
Notes: A transport equivalent of the S-61B (see page 283)
with sonar, weapons, and automatic blade folding deleted,
and a cargo floor inserted, the S-61A is used by the USAF
for missile site support as the CH-3B, this having 1,250 shp
T58-GE-8Bs and accommodation for 26 troops or 15
stretchers. Eight similarly-powered S-61A-1s supplied to
Denmark for the rescue task were supplemented in 1970 by
a ninth machine, and 10 T58-GE-5-powered S-61A-4s
equipped to carry 31 combat troops and supplied to
Malaysia are being supplemented during 1971 by six further
S-61A-4s. The S-61L and S-61N (see 1967 edition) are
non-amphibious and amphibious commercial versions.

SIKORSKY S-61R

Country of Origin: USA.

Type: Amphibious transport and rescue helicopter.

Power Plant: (CH-3E) Two 1,500 shp General Electric T58-GE-5 turboshafts.

Performance: (CH-3E at 21,247 lb/9 635 kg) Max. speed, 162 mph (261 km/h) at sea level; range cruise, 144 mph (232 km/h); max. inclined climb, 1,310 ft/min (6,6 m/sec); hovering ceiling (in ground effect), 4,100 ft (1 250 m); range with 10% reserves, 465 mls (748 km).

Weights: (CH-3E) Empty, 13,255 lb (6 010 kg); normal take-off, 21,247 lb (9 635 kg); max. take-off, 22,050 lb (10 000 kg).

Dimensions: Rotor diam, 62 ft 0 in (18,90 m); fuselage length, 57 ft 3 in (17,45 m).

Notes: Although based on the S-61A, the S-61R embodies numerous design changes, including a rear ramp and a tricycle-type undercarriage. Initial model for the USAF was the CH-3C with 1,300 shp T58-GE-1 turboshafts, but this was subsequently updated to CH-3E standards. The CH-3E can accommodate 25–30 troops or 5,000 lb (2 270 kg) of cargo, and may be fitted with a TAT-102 barbette on each sponson mounting a 7,62-mm Minigun. The HH-3E (illustrated) is a USAF rescue version with armour, self-sealing tanks, and refuelling probe, and the HH-3F Pelican is a US Coast Guard search and rescue model.

SIKORSKY S-62A

Country of Origin: USA.

Type: Amphibious utility transport helicopter.

Power Plant: One 1,250 shp General Electric CT58-110-1 turboshaft.

Performance: Max. speed, 101 mph (163 km/h) at sea level; max. cruise, 92 mph (148 km/h); max. inclined climb, 1,140 ft/min (5,8 m/sec); hovering ceiling (in ground effect), 14,100 ft (4 295 m), (out of ground effect), 4,600 ft (1 400 m); range with 10% reserves, 462 mls (743 km).

Weights: Empty equipped, 4,957 lb (2 248 kg); max. take-off, 7,900 lb (3 583 kg).

Dimensions: Rotor diam, 53 ft 0 in (16,16 m); fuselage length, 44 ft $6\frac{1}{2}$ in (13,58 m).

Notes: The S-62 embodies many components of the piston-engined S-55 (see 1961 edition), including rotor blades and heads, and the basic model is the S-62A which can accommodate 12 troops or 10 airline passengers. The S-62A is licence-built in Japan by Mitsubishi for both military and civil roles, both the Maritime and Air Self-Defence Forces using this type in the rescue role. A US Coast Guard rescue version is designated HH-52A (see 1970 edition), this having a rescue platform, and automatic stabilisation and towing equipment. The HH-52A operates at higher weights, the S-62C being the commercial and military foreign version.

SIKORSKY S-64 SKYCRANE

Country of Origin: USA.

Type: Heavy flying-crane helicopter.

Power Plant: Two 4,500 shp Pratt & Whitney T73-P-1 turboshafts.

Performance: (CH-54A at 38,000 lb/17 237 kg) Max. speed, 127 mph (204 km/h) at sea level; max. cruise, 109 mph (175 km/h); max. inclined climb, 1,700 ft/min (8,64 m/sec); hovering ceiling (in ground effect), 10,600 ft (3 230 m), (out of ground effect), 6,900 ft (2 100 m); range, 253 mls (407 km).

Weights: (CH-54A) Empty, 19,234 lb (8 724 kg); max. take-off, 42,000 lb (19 050 kg).

Dimensions: Rotor diam, 72 ft 0 in (21,95 m); fuselage length, 70 ft 3 in (21,41 m).

Notes: The S-64A serves with the US Army as the CH-54A Tarhe in the heavy lift role, and may be fitted with a 15,000-lb (6 800-kg) hoist or an all-purpose pod (seen fitted above) which can accommodate 45 troops or 24 casualty stretchers. The commercial equivalent of the CH-54A is designated S-64E. A developed version, the CH-54B powered by T73-P-700 turboshafts of 4,800 shp, was flown on June 30, 1969, other changes including dual mainwheels and an increase in max. take-off to 47,000 lb (21 319 kg). The CH-54B also features a new gearbox and high-lift rotor blades, the civil equivalent being the S-64F.

SIKORSKY S-65

Country of Origin: USA.

Type: Heavy assault transport helicopter.

Power Plant: Two 3,925 shp General Electric T64-GE-413 turboshafts.

Performance: Max. speed, 196 mph (315 km/h) at sea level; max. cruise, 173 mph (278 km/h); max. inclined climb, 2,180 ft/min (11,08 m/sec); hovering ceiling (in ground effect), 13,400 ft (4 080 m), (out of ground effect), 6,500 ft (1 980 m); range, 257 mls (413 km).

Weights: Empty, 23,485 lb (10 653 kg); normal take-off, 36,400 lb (16 510 kg); 42,000 lb (19 050 kg).

Dimensions: Rotor diam, 72 ft 3 in (22,02 m); fuselage length, 67 ft 2 in (20,47 m).

Notes: Using many components based on those of the S-64 (see page 279), the S-65 can accommodate 38 combat troops or 24 casualty stretchers and four medical attendants. The initial US Navy version, the CH-53A Sea Stallion, has 2,850 shp T64-GE-6 turboshafts, and the HH-53B for the USAF is similar apart from having 3,080 shp T64-GE-3s, a flight refuelling probe, jettisonable auxiliary tanks and armament, the HH-53C differing primarily in having 3,435 shp T64-GE-7s and an external cargo hook. The US Marine Corps' CH-53D (to which the specification applies) has up-rated engines and can carry up to 64 troops. The CH-53DG for Federal Germany (illustrated) is similar.

SIKORSKY S-67 BLACKHAWK

Country of Origin: USA.

Type: Two-seat attack helicopter.

Power Plant: Two 1,500 shp General Electric T58-GE-5 turboshafts.

Performance: (Estimated) Max. speed, 205 mph (330 km/h) at sea level; max. cruise, 195 mph (314 km/h); normal range, 250 mls (402 km).

Weights: Empty, 10,900 lb (4 944 kg); max. take-off (attack configuration), 18,500 lb (8 392 kg); max. overload take-off, 22,000 lb (9 979 kg).

Dimensions: Rotor diam, 62 ft 0 in (18,90 m); fuselage length, 64 ft 4¾ in (19,63 m).

Notes: The S-67 is a company-funded development based on the unsuccessful S-66 entry in the US Army's AAFSS (Advanced Aerial Fire Support System) competition, and rotors, gearboxes, drive shafts, and controls are similar to those of the S-61. As an attack helicopter the S-67 will carry up to 8,000 lb (3 629 kg) of ordnance, including barbette-mounted 7,62-mm Miniguns, 20-mm or 30-mm cannon, or 40-mm grenade launchers, and the 28-ft (8,53-m) fixed wing carries speed brakes to increase combat manoeuvrability. With some cabin modifications the S-67 could transport 15 troops a distance of 220 mls (354 km) at 165 mph (265 km/h), and for the rescue role with auxiliary fuel could fly distances up to 600 mls (966 km).

WESTLAND WG.13 LYNX

Country of Origin: United Kingdom.
Type: Multi-purpose and transport helicopter.
Power Plant: Two 900 shp Rolls-Royce BS.360-07-26 turboshafts.
Performance: (Estimated) Max. speed, 184 mph (296 km/h) at sea level; max. cruise, 161 mph (259 km/h); max. inclined climb, 2,500 ft/min (12,7 m/sec); max. range with 10 passengers, 173 mls (278 km), with max. standard fuel and 5% reserves, 495 mls (796 km).
Weights: Empty, 4,920 lb (2 232 kg); empty equipped (average), 5,750 lb (2 812 kg); max. take-off, 8,000 lb (3 620 kg).
Dimensions: Rotor diam, 42 ft 0 in (12,80 m); fuselage length, 40 ft 6 in (12,34 m).
Notes: The Lynx, the first of 12 prototypes of which was scheduled to commence its flight test programme in January 1971, is one of the three types covered by the Anglo-French helicopter agreement, and production deliveries (to the British Army) are scheduled to commence in the autumn of 1973. To the end of 1980 a total of 277 is programmed for supply to the British armed forces, and current plans call for some 80 examples of an ASW version for France's *Aéronavale* from 1975. The standard Lynx will carry 12 combat troops, up to 2,738 lb (1 242 kg) of freight internally, or a slung load of up to 3,000 lb (1 361 kg).

WESTLAND (S-61B) SEA KING

Country of Origin: United Kingdom (US licence).
Type: Amphibious anti-submarine helicopter.
Power Plant: Two 1,500 shp Rolls-Royce Gnome H.1400 turboshafts.
Performance: (At 20,500 lb/9 298 kg) Max. speed, 143 mph (230 km/h); max. cruise, 131 mph (211 km/h); max. endurance cruise, 86 mph (138 km/h); max. inclined climb, 1,770 ft/min (8,97 m/sec); max. range with standard fuel, 690 mls (1 110 km).
Weights: Basic, 12,700 lb (5 760 kg); empty equipped, 15,474 lb (7 019 kg); max. take-off, 21,500 lb (9 751 kg).
Dimensions: Rotor diam, 62 ft 0 in (18,90 m); fuselage length, 54 ft 9 in (16,69 m).
Notes: The Sea King H.A.S. Mk. 1 is an anglicised licence-built version of the Sikorsky S-61B and, apart from equipment, is essentially similar to the US Navy's SH-3D Sea King (see 1968 edition), the Gnome turboshafts being licence-produced derivatives of the General Electric T58. Sixty Westland-built Sea Kings are being delivered to the Royal Navy, 22 have been ordered by Federal Germany, 10 by Norway and six by India. The SH-3A (1,250 shp T58-GE-8B) serves with Canada (CHSS-2) and is licence-built by Mitsubishi, and the SH-3D (1,400 shp T58-GE-10) serves with Italy, Brazil and Spain. The SH-3D is manufactured under licence in Italy by Agusta.

ACKNOWLEDGEMENTS

The author wishes to record his thanks to David Dorrell, John W. R. Taylor, and F. G. Swanborough for their assistance in obtaining some of the photographs included in this edition. The sources of copyright photographs appearing on these pages are as follows: *Aireview*, pages 172, 261, 268, 278; Karl-Heinz Eyermann, 24; *Flight*, 132; Howard Levy, 18; Ronaldo Olive, 86, 88; Stephen Peltz, 22, 26, 42, 130, 152, 194, 210, 263, 273, 277; Hans Redemann, 234, 244, 271; E. J. Riding, 184; Tass, 40, 162, 164, 230, 242.

INDEX OF AIRCRAFT TYPES

285

287